*Patrick Swayze riding horse, posed at a portrait session 1990.*

**"I think we all need to remember that dreams are the fabric of the future and if you believe in those dreams, you can make them happen or re-discover an old dream. And just believe in yourself. And spread the love!"**
**—Patrick Swayze, November 27, 2005**
*Used with permission of the Official Patrick Swayze International Fan Club*

Patrick Swayze, the beloved dancer, actor, singer, songwriter, producer, choreographer, family man, athlete, horseman, and more, had a diversified career in the arts world for over thirty-five years. He often played hero roles in his work and spoke about traditional values such as honor, integrity, morality, passion, faith, and love. He was always searching for meaning in his life and trying to give to others some joy or sense of purpose or meaning. During his hard-fought and inspirational battle against pancreatic cancer, he became a real-life hero to millions of people. Patrick Swayze was taken too soon, but his remarkable spirit and enormous legacy will always shine bright.

Discover how his focus on dreams for himself and others sustained him and guided him to live a zest-filled and hopeful life even while dealing with great adversity. Honor and celebrate Patrick while reading about his career, his connection with his family, and his involvement in advocacy for dance, cancer advances, and conservation. Learn what his professional colleagues and fans have to say about him. Finally, get a look at what I think Patrick would say to us now.

ALSO BY SUE TABASHNIK

*The Fans' Love Story:*
*How the Movie* DIRTY DANCING *Captured the Hearts of Millions!*

*The Fans' Love Story ENCORE:*
*How the Movie* DIRTY DANCING *Captured the Hearts of Millions!*

*Dear Yvonne,*
*Thank you so much*
*for the support at*
*work & of my writing!*
*Let us be like Patrick*

# PATRICK SWAYZE
## The Dreamer

### SUE TABASHNIK

*Follow our dreams!*

*All my best wishes,*

*Sue T.*

PASSION
SPIRIT
DREAMS
PRESS

**Walled Lake, Michigan**

## The Fans' Love Story ENCORE: How the Movie DIRTY DANCING Captured the Hearts of Millions!

"A celebratory text packed with behind-the-scenes information on the producers, stars, and film team that includes an in-depth interview from producer Linda Gottlieb about its making, interviews and photos with story consultant and dancer Jackie Horner, and more. . . . Film history as well as general-interest collections will find this a fascinating, specific overview of not just how the movie was made, but the process whereby it was marketed to eventually reach millions of enthusiasts."

—D. Donovan, Senior eBook Reviewer, MBR

"Wow! What a job you did. Just fabulous. Love you—love the book. I now will cherish it and all of our memories."

—Jackie Horner, Story Consultant, Dirty Dancing, New York

"Congratulations, kudos, and BRAVO. . . . We thank you for your generous pages of sharing what was a lifetime adventure for us. We love reading it and consider it to be part of our history to pass along to the generations that follow in our family. DD is still a topic of interest and fascination with folks . . . You have certainly given voice and insight for those who can't get enough!"

—Patt and Tom Rocks,
Dance extras on the Lake Lure Dirty Dancing set, South Carolina

"A must for any Dirty Dancing fan. A wonderful tribute to Dirty Dancing and Patrick Swayze. The book is very well-written, beautifully laid out with great pictures that capture such a spirit of the film. It gives fascinating insight as to how the film was made. Sue has done another great job, a fabulous, highly recommended book."

—Jane Brazier, United Kingdom

"She did an absolutely wonderful tribute to the film and Patrick, as well as the cast. I think Patrick would be very proud of what she's done here. This book is a great behind-the-scenes story about the filming of the movie, as well as the aftermath. . . . This book will make you want to sit down and watch the movie once again, with a whole new perspective. . . . Thank you for the 'Time of My Life'!"

—*Holly Tuell, Wisconsin*

### *The Fans' Love Story: How the Movie* DIRTY DANCING *Captured the Hearts of Millions!*

"Your book is both great journalism and original writing. It is a very positive testament to Patrick and his life as an Artist and the impact it had on others."

—*Joshua Sinclair, Director, Writer, Producer of* Jump!, *Austria*

"Patrick Swayze captured the hearts of millions with *Dirty Dancing* twenty years ago. *The Fans' Love Story: How the Movie* DIRTY DANCING *Captured the Hearts of Millions!* explores the fans' fascination with the work and how it made them life-long fans of Swayze and the film. As Sue Tabashnik interviews fans to get an idea of why the film gained so much popularity, and much more, *The Fans' Love Story* is of strong interest to any fan of the film, highly recommended."

—*Midwest Book Review*

"Thank you from the bottom of my heart for introducing me to so many people who share my depth of connection to Baby, Johnny, and the entire *Dirty Dancing* experience."

—*Debbie Wallerstein, Florida*

"The interviews with the people involved in the film are fantastic and give you a rare glimpse into the world of *Dirty Dancing* and the Catskills. The book also reminds us all of that magical moment when we found our first love. Feel the magic of the movie again and see how it touched and continues to touch lives all over the world."

—*Jan Griffith, Texas*

"Every *Dirty Dancing* or Patrick Swayze fan will want this book. It is filled with insights on the movie and Patrick from many different perspectives. Personal accounts from people behind the scenes along with photos of the movie location give the reader a sense of being there. Fans' comments and personal observations from people who were there during production help to round out this wonderful reading experience and brings fans a little closer to knowing Patrick as a person."

—*Ingrid Mennella, Florida*

# PATRICK SWAYZE
## *The Dreamer*

In memory of my grandmother, Leah Tabashnik, and Patrick Swayze:
A portion of the proceeds from the sale of this book will be
donated to the Patrick Swayze Pancreas Cancer Research Fund
at the Stanford Cancer Institute.

ISBN 978-0-9894086-3-9 (paperback)

ISBN 978-0-9894086-4-6 (ebook)

PRINTED IN THE UNITED STATES OF AMERICA

FRONT COVER PHOTO CREDIT: Greg Gorman/Contour by Getty Images. *Patrick Swayze is photographed for* Venice Magazine *on June 1, 2004.*

Book and cover design: Patricia Bacall, www.bacallcreative.com

*To my Mom,*
*Phyllis Friedman,*

*To my Dad,*
*David Tabashnik,*

*Forever in my heart!*

## ACKNOWLEDGMENT
## OF GRATITUDE

*To Mr. Patrick Swayze,*

Rest in peace,
knowing that you indeed continue
to make a difference in the world.

# CONTENTS

# INTRODUCTION

Why write a book on Patrick Swayze? I think that there are millions of people who consider Patrick a hero and that there is a huge legacy of work and spirit of Patrick that lives on. If you have any doubt about it, look on Facebook, where photo after photo is found on a daily basis on multiple sites from all over the world. This phenomenon multiplies more than tenfold on occasions like Patrick's birthday or anniversary of his death. One will find messages saying people cannot believe that Patrick has passed, that people are still sad and crying regarding his death, that people are sorely missing him, and that his work is still immensely enjoyed. Simply put, people just cannot get enough of Patrick! It is as if these photos and messages are tributes to Patrick and keep him alive, so to speak, and are a means to hang on to Patrick's zest-filled, hopeful philosophy and way of life. I really think that the key to Patrick's appeal to so many people is his focus on dreams for himself and dreams for others.

I hope that this book captures the essence of Patrick's wonderful outlook on life, which has such an inspiring emphasis on dreams, and thus will perpetuate this spirituality in a world where it is so desperately needed. And what better way is there to celebrate and honor Patrick!

I am very grateful to Patrick for the multitude of press and appearances that he did, as this, in addition to his voluminous work as an Artist, is a wonderful remembrance of him. The wealth of media on Patrick, the information provided by Patrick to the Official Patrick Swayze International Fan Club, and my experiences of meeting Patrick and some of his family all have enabled me to create this homage to Patrick.

Credit: Official Patrick Swayze International Fan Club.

*Patrick Swayze and wife, Lisa Niemi, give a video holiday message to the fans on November 27, 2005 in London.*

## CHAPTER ONE

## DREAMS:
### Early Beginnings and Influences

**Lisa: Merry Christmas.**

**Patrick: And a Happy New Year to all our fans. We want you to know that we really appreciate you and really love you for staying behind us for so long. Hopefully we will continue to entice, incite, intimidate, and inspire.**

**Lisa: And all the most incredibly wonderful things for 2006. . . .**

**Patrick: I think we all need to remember that dreams are the fabric of the future and if you believe in those dreams, you can make them happen or re-discover an old dream. And just believe in yourself. And spread the love!**

The above excerpt is from a video interview that Patrick Swayze and his wife, Lisa Niemi, gave to Margaret Howden, the president of the Official Patrick Swayze International Fan Club, on November 27, 2005, as a holiday message to the fans. First of all, this was just typical generosity and graciousness of Patrick to be available to his fans and to thank his fans for their support. Patrick and Lisa were in London for the world premiere of the movie *Keeping Mum*, in which Patrick played the role of Lance, a lecherous golf pro. In addition to Patrick and Lisa creating the London holiday video for fans, Patrick's PA gave the fan club the time and place for fans to go to see and be greeted by Patrick as he arrived for the premiere screening of *Keeping Mum*.

The second key point regarding the video is Patrick's focus on pursuing dreams, which is really an important part of Patrick's philosophy of the way he lived his life personally and professionally, and has become a wonderful legacy to the world.

Patrick's determination and focus on achieving his dreams started when he was quite young. Patrick was interviewed by Donny Deutsch on the May 25, 2005 episode of the CNBC television show *The Big Idea with Donny Deutsch*. Patrick spoke about having endured being frequently beaten up as a kid (was even put in the hospital one time) while growing up in Texas because he was in the arts—a dancer, a violinist, a performer. He talked about how he had tried various ways to stop the bullying, including giving up the arts. However, nothing that he did differently worked, so he stopped trying to fit in and decided he was going to do what he wanted to do. Patrick told Donny Deutsch:

**Actually, at age thirteen, I made a big decision, you know, when it didn't change anything for me, I decided, no one's ever going to stop me from what I believe in or my dreams for as long as I live.**

Furthermore, I think that probably by the age of thirteen, the belief in hard work and a strong work ethic with passion—learned from his mother, Patsy, and father, Jesse, and the belief that you never give up, learned from his father—were lessons already deeply ingrained in Patrick. It seems like these two principles were used by Patrick throughout his life personally and professionally to deal with adversity and to achieve dreams.

During an interview with Alex Simon, "PATRICK SWAYZE: PEACEFUL WARRIOR" in *Venice Magazine* in June 2004, Patrick spoke about the strong, diverse, positive influence of his mother and father on him that began early in his life and always stayed with him in all aspects of his life. Patrick commented about his father, Jesse Swayze, who had ranching (including being a state champion calf-roper) in his background and whose profession was engineering:

> He really taught me so many things that in your younger years are kind of cliché, but as you get older, you realize their importance: like integrity, passion, in your work ethic. I now live my life by most of the things my dad taught me. I think my favorite saying of his would be: "All I got is my integrity. To this day, I ain't never seen a hearse pulling a U-Haul."

Patrick talked about his mother, Patsy Swayze, who was a world-renowned dancer and choreographer, in the same interview:

> That's the other side of me: the intensity, the passion, the drive, the belief in communicating something through the arts. It's all those qualities of my mother's that have really led me down all these tangential paths in my life. My parents were an amazing couple.

Used with permission.

*The Swayze Men: Brothers (top, from left) Patrick, Don, and Sean horsing around with their father, Jesse Swayze (center).*

Credit: Deborah Feingold/Corbis Premium Historical/Getty Images.

*Patrick Swayze and his mother, Patsy Swayze, 1988.*

## CHAPTER TWO

## CAREER

When Patrick sustained a severe injury to his left knee while playing football during his senior year of high school on October 31, 1970, he used his grit, determination, and strong desire to achieve his dreams to get through the ordeal of surgery and rehab. After the injury forced him to give up playing football, he actually went on to another dream, gymnastics. Then after yet another injury to his left knee while training in gymnastics for the Olympics, he left that dream and went on to another dream. He became a professional dancer for many years, while often having to deal with aggravation and injury of the knee, which involved severe pain, more surgery, and multiple procedures. Finally, in around 1976, due to the knee problem, Patrick pursued another dream, that of being an actor. And the rest is history.

Regarding his determination to be an accomplished actor, Patrick was known to say that the key to his success in getting acting roles and progressing as an actor was that he worked harder than other people. Patrick's strong desire to accomplish his dreams was well known to be fueled by his strong work ethic, which as discussed earlier, he certainly got at least partly from his mother, a consummate dance professional, choreographer, and teacher. Patsy started taking Patrick to work to her progressive dance school in Texas when he was just a baby and started teaching him dance at the age of three. Patrick spoke to Gavin Esler on the BBC *HARDtalk Extra* in 2006 about his return to the stage in the role of Nathan Detroit in the London production of *Guys and Dolls*. He talked about how there is nothing like the stage and his early start into the arts:

**I was literally born under the stage, grew up with kings and queens and giants and fairies and goblins being my babysitters. Sleeping in theater seats from the time I was little 'cause my mother is a choreographer, so she's choreographed just about every musical ever written.**

It is well-documented that Patsy had very high hopes for Patrick to succeed in the arts world. Furthermore, it is mentioned that Patrick thought that on the one hand, his mother ingrained in him the value of working hard, but on the other hand, this may have contributed to him being very self-critical and to sometimes thinking that he was not good enough. Patrick spoke about dealing with these "demons" in a positive way and not blaming anyone else for having them.

Patrick always worked extremely hard by initially taking acting lessons with Warren Robertson and Milton Katselas, analyzing each character he was playing from multiple angles, arduously researching and training for his character portrayal, and giving way beyond one hundred percent of himself to his role. Patrick did whatever he could to develop his acting skills and be taken seriously as an actor. He initially downplayed his dance abilities and turned down film deals that offered a lot of money because to Patrick it seemed like they were stereotyping him as a sex symbol, rather than treating him as an earnest actor.

In "Patrick Swayze: 'Dancing' on top of the world," Joe Leydon, Houston film critic, writes in his spring 1983 interview of Patrick:

**He wants to be a star, he concedes, but on his own terms: Not as a teeny-bopper idol, not as a slab of TV beefcake, but as a serious actor.**

Joe Leydon focuses on Patrick initially not using his dancing skills in movies in an August 19, 1987 interview:

**But Swayze has tamed a few of the demons that once nipped at his heels as he ran toward stardom. In fact, by agreeing to**

star in *Dirty Dancing*, he actually exorcised an old fear about his professional image.

[Patrick:] "If I had started doing musicals and dance films right when I'd started out," he believes, "my vote would have been cancelled. Maybe critics in major cities would have heralded it. But from a small-town point of view, from the people who buy the tickets, they would not have understood it. . . ."

But after a series of straight dramatic parts, Swayze felt it was safe for him to put on his dancing shoes, to play the sexy Johnny Castle in *Dirty Dancing*. [Patrick:] "It's interesting, the way people look at things," he says. "If I'd done it then, and then tried to be taken seriously as an actor, it would have been, Oh. Dancer turns actor. But now, it's, Oh. Actor with other talents.

I did *Dirty Dancing* because it was my opportunity for the first time on film to dance. And, it would wash better with the world, in that the dancing was something like an introductory course to, quote, Patrick Swayze fans, unquote, that wouldn't be alienating."

Linda Gottlieb, producer of *Dirty Dancing*, shares in my November 17, 2012 interview how it came to be that Patrick was cast in the film:

As to Patrick, I had known about Patrick some years ago because I had been working in the industry and had been thinking about doing a film involving ballet (which, for various reasons, I didn't do). In the course of the research as to who could play the lead in that film, I had discovered that Patrick had been trained as a classical ballet dancer. So I suggested him to our casting agent, Bonnie Timmermann. We screened everything he had done. We brought him in, and we, of course, loved him.

In case anyone has any doubt regarding Patrick being the only one asked to play the male lead in *Dirty Dancing*, Eleanor Bergstein, Writer and Co-Producer of *Dirty Dancing*, sets the record straight in a January 25, 2017 interview with Randee Dawn from TODAY.com and with comments made March 13, 2017, to me:

**The only actor ever offered the role of Johnny (Castle) was Patrick Swayze. "Out of the woodwork actors come out now and say they turned it down, but that's not true," she says. "I told (Swayze), 'If you decide not to do this, I don't think I can make this movie.'**

**"We were looking for a hooded quality in the eyes. We were looking through head shots and saw Patrick and I said 'those eyes are what I mean,' and Emile (Director of *Dirty Dancing*) said, 'As a matter of fact he's a Joffrey Dancer.' Luckily Emile knew that from the dance world, because when we turned his resume over, there wasn't any dancing on it, he'd taken it off. So it was Patrick, always Patrick."**

In the BBC *HARDtalk Extra* interview, Patrick talked about how his dance background and growing up in Texas contributed to his success in the performing arts:

**The dance world teaches you something. . . . The concept of: Suffer for your art. Pay your dues. And then it takes me into Texas clichés: Only the strong survive. Nobody said it was going to be easy. If it's worth having, it's worth working for. I live by these things in my life.**

Patrick used some of the above clichés to work very hard to get the role of Sam Wheat in *Ghost*. He was adamant about getting an audition even though Jerry Zucker, the director, was not keen to see him. During the audition, he was willing to read multiple scenes to convince people that he was the right actor for the role. Patrick's tactics obviously worked really well. It is said that his heartfelt audition performance was so good that it had some of the people in the room in tears, including Jerry Zucker.

One example of Patrick again working hard and turning adversity into a positive was how Patrick auditioned to get the role of Vida Boheme in *To Wong Foo, Thanks for Everything! Julie Newmar.* From the *US Weekly* PATRICK SWAYZE interview in September 1995 by Tom O'Neill:

> **Like Zucker, Kidron had been reluctant to meet Swayze but was instantly persuaded by his audition—which, this time, was a little unusual. Instead of reading from the script, the actor arrived in drag and delivered an improvised 45-minute monologue drawing from his painful boyhood memories of getting beaten up by the town bullies for being a ballet dancer.**

> **"I hope the world rewards him for this performance," says Kidron, who admits to being astounded at the lengths Swayze was willing to go to reach the emotional core of his character. "He does have these doubts, these demons, these agonies," she says, "and he uses them as leverage to get a performance."**

On a lighter note, in the September 1995 article by Joe Leydon, "Patrick Swayze: Getting in touch with his feminine side as a most womanly woman in '*To Wong Foo*,'" the Houston film critic wrote:

> **Kidron insists that, when it came to casting Swayze, the actor's appropriateness for the part wasn't merely skin deep.**

> **"I think Patrick has a humanity and an emotional quality that I thought would give the serious end of the movie a push," she says. "But I'll be honest—I needed someone who looked good, too. I don't think the movie would have worked if Vida looked like the back end of a bus."**

**Swayze accepts the compliment with a hearty laugh, and a tongue-in-cheeky boast: "I *am* the prettiest, beyond a shadow of a doubt. I have elegance, I have sophistication, and I have class. What other of them bitches has that?"**

Patrick did receive a Golden Globe nomination for his performances in *Ghost* and *To Wong Foo, Thanks for Everything! Julie Newmar*, and also for his performance as Johnny Castle in *Dirty Dancing*.

Another example of Patrick working really hard and putting his soul into his work was the prepping he did for his role as Dr. Max Lowe in *City of Joy*, which was filmed in India. It is reported that he worked for several days in Mother Teresa's hospice for the dying and home for lepers. And of course, Patrick honed skydiving and surfing skills to play Bodhi in *Point Break*. He had military training to perform his roles as Kevin Scott in *Uncommon Valor* and Jim Lance in *Green Dragon*, and also learned the Vietnamese language for the latter film.

Patrick often talked about how he reinvented and refocused his acting career many times.

Once again, regarding wanting to develop his acting skills as much as possible, he remarked to Joe Leydon, Houston film critic, in September 1995:

**But I really am hellbent to see how far I can take this craft of acting. . . .**

**My battle is, "Can I be the kind of actor that I want to be?" I don't care how you try to box me in. I'm going to break your picture of me. And it's going to be fun doing it. Every time you think you've got me pegged, I'm going to surprise you.**

**I'm having a great time, because I'm getting to do what I want to do. And I feel very grateful that I got out of being sucked into that hit machine mentality. Of course I want**

hits. Of course I want movies that make money. Just so I can keep getting the license to do what I want to do. But I know that if I live from that point of view, my work will start falling down.

On September 29, 2005, Patrick spoke to Mark Shanahan from the *Boston Globe* about staying true to the craft of acting:

**Q: Why not reprise the role of Johnny Castle?**

**A: I would, but Hollywood wants to formulize everything. I'm staying true to the craft, trying to get closer to the word "artist." It was the soulful part of *Dirty Dancing* that translated for people. When you add heat to soul, that's when you really have something.**

As a side note, it was reported in the media (not known whether it is true or not) that Patrick also had insisted that members of the original *Dirty Dancing* team had to be included in any remake of *Dirty Dancing*.

On November 25, 2005, Patrick was asked by Xav Judd, in an interview published by 6degreesfilm.com, how he chooses his movie parts:

**Q: How do you decide which film roles to take?**

**A: It's hard to find any kind of story or project that hasn't been done before. The key is the slant, the direction that the vision is coming from. And as you go along you start realising that you want to be in control of that vision. As you do this for a lot of years, you wake up one day and realise "what's wrong with me, why don't I direct, why don't I produce?" My vision might be as interesting as someone else's. And there are many times when, the longer you do this, you start getting faith in your abilities to look at a script and know what needs to be fixed. So I just look for something**

different. I kind of live for the goose bump test. It's really hard to find anything that isn't trash, and it's amazing how much money people have out there to offer you for crap.

On November 27, 2005, in the London interview given to the Official Patrick Swayze International Fan Club, Patrick talked about transitioning into a mature leading man:

I just realised that this is an exciting place in my life. I've done movies that have really affected people on so many levels—it's given me an inspiration for this next phase of my life. Can I really pull off turning into a Mature Leading Man? That's what *King Solomon's Mines* and *Icon* was for me. My experiment of (in a deep voice) "Patrick Swayze in the man role" and I thought I was going to be bored with it. I thought I was going to hate it but I was like "No, I like the wild man!" I liked the guy out there that's totally unpredictable and you don't know what the hell he's going to do next!

So, I don't know if you noticed, but in *King Solomon's Mines* although I do a really good job, there's a little bit of "playing the hero." Even though I'm really proud of it, and then you watch *Icon* really quickly after it, if you've studied it, *Icon* is much more me—the Patrick Swayze in his own body. It was a bit of growth for me, a big step for me. When I saw them (the two miniseries), I like them on me . . .

In these later years, which also coincided with getting alcohol out of his life (after 1993 or so), Patrick said that he purposively stepped away from the blockbuster mentality and took on many roles in independent films.

Thus, a key principle that Patrick emphasized throughout his career as an actor, that he used to develop his craft, was personal and spiritual growth. He spoke to Barbara Walters, in the famous post-*Dirty Dancing*, May 11, 1988, ABC *Barbara Walters Special Interview* about him saying no to "teenage idol" movie roles. He explained his reason for rejecting those parts was that he thought he could eventually be taken as a serious actor after he sustained enough personal growth and experience.

In addition, here is another important, what I will call a personal, spiritual philosophy of Patrick, which served him well throughout his personal life and career, quoted in the 1988 book *PATRICK SWAYZE* by Mitchell Krugel:

**Very early I learned that you have to be true to yourself about what you care about—what you believe in. If you're not, you have nothing at all. You have to listen to that little bird inside that tells you what's right.**

Regarding formal religious upbringing, Patrick was born and raised Catholic, but he actually studied many religions and philosophies, including EST, Buddhism, Transcendental Meditation, the Koran, and Scientology. He was also known to dabble with crystals. Patrick was asked by an interviewer from HollywoodTV.com on June 18, 2007, what he did to develop himself spiritually. He replied that he became a Mahayana Buddhist a long time ago. He also spoke about how important it was to him to research different belief systems and reasons people hold on to faith and hope. He said he incorporated his research findings into his belief system.

Patrick spoke to Karl J. Paloucek on June 6, 2004, about his meaningful experience in Africa during the shooting of the Hallmark television mini-series *King Solomon Mines*:

**The people really affected me. How simple and honest things could be, he says. We kind of get ruined in the Western world of thinking that the brass ring is what's important, when it's very simple things in life that are important like hanging on to faith and hope.**

In the 1995 interview by *US Weekly*, Patrick was asked about any keepsakes (besides his father's knife) that he had. He said:

**This is my keepsake *[holds up an emerald-and-crystal-encrusted scepter]*. It's my magic wand. It has been in the hands of holy men in India and Japan and all over the world. I put it into each person's hand and say this to bless the production and create an atmosphere of mutual goals devoid of ego.**

In this same 1995 *US Weekly* interview, the interviewer asked Patrick if he ever was concerned about what people would think of his image due to his spirituality, including his wand. While you ponder Patrick's response to the question, keep in mind that 1995 was the year that *To Wong Foo, Thanks for Everything! Julie Newmar* (Patrick played a drag queen) and *Three Wishes* (Patrick played a spiritual drifter) were released. Patrick said:

**I don't care what image I have! Take any image you want of me. I'm going to change it, because we are chameleons. We have the crazy person, the shy person, the angry person, the intellectual person, the ignorant person, the gay person, we have the little boy in us, the little girl in us . . . Oh! Heaven forbid we have a feminine side! I've now ceased to worry about image, because I don't care what people think of me anymore. Because I've had such a battle with what *I* think of me and with trying to find a way to like myself.**

Along similar lines, Patrick stated to Joe Leydon, Houston film critic, in a September 3, 1995 interview:

**It's like, not a whole lot of men would be willing to play a drag queen. Because very few of us are comfortable with our masculinity. We're always trying to prove something. I know that real well, because I've spent half of my life trying to prove something. I don't know what it was I was trying to prove—that I was worthy, or that I was more than what I looked like, or what I could do with my body. I've also**

accepted that I am a wild man, and that's not a bad thing. It's a bad thing only if you screw your life up with it. But it can give you an edge, and give you a focus, and give you a passion when the world wants to suck the passion out of you.

Patrick told Tom O'Neill in the *US Weekly* interview in September 1995 about starring in *To Wong Foo, Thanks for Everything! Julie Newmar*:

It's not so much about trying to make a transition as about wanting more and more challenges. I mean, leading men get boring and one-dimensional real fast, and I'm not a person that can be satisfied. I've gotta keep trying to see if I can better myself as a person and an actor.

As mentioned earlier, Patrick played a very spiritual character, Jack McCloud, in the 1995 movie, *Three Wishes*. The director of *Three Wishes*, Martha Coolidge, indicated that Patrick brought to his role his very extensive philosophic background and strong spirituality, along with his athleticism and ability to work with children and animals.

In a very different role as Dalton in the film *Road House*, Patrick played a bar bouncer, which showcased a combination of philosophy and extreme physicality. Regarding Patrick and the Dalton character he portrayed, Alex Simon in "Great Conversations: Patrick Swayze" on June 10, 2015 wrote:

In fact, he closely resembled Dalton, his character in this writer's all-time guilty pleasure, Rowdy Herrington's *Road House* (1989), as a bar bouncer with a Master's in Philosophy from NYU, who could quote Confucius and snap necks in near-perfect synchronicity.

Patrick also spoke to Alex Simon in his *Venice Magazine* June 2004 interview about the complexity of the character and his peaceful warrior philosophy that he brought to his Dalton *Road House* performance:

**The whole basis of *Road House* was a modern-day western with the lead character being quite a complicated man. . . . And I liked the fact that it was one of the first opportunities for me to put out there my passion for being a peaceful warrior: to be highly-skilled, but to avoid violence or hurting another human being at all costs, unless you have no choice.**

In *Dirty Dancing* (1987), as the character of Johnny Castle, it seems that Patrick drew on his personal quest to find his place in the world to make that very real for his portrayal of Johnny Castle's similar quest. In addition, Patrick told Bobbie Wygant, a long-time entertainment reporter and critic with NBC 5 KXAS-TV Channel 5 Dallas/Fort Worth, in a 1987 interview regarding *Dirty Dancing*:

**I feel it really turned out to be a wonderful movie for kids from the point of view of making your dreams come true and not allowing mommy and daddy and society to tell you to give them up.**

Furthermore, Patrick told the Telegraph.co.uk on September 23, 2006, his take on why *Dirty Dancing* has been so successful:

**It has been so successful because basically it's about love, and how the power of love can redeem us all.**

Of course, his sentimental, famous parting line as the character of Sam Wheat in the 1990 movie *Ghost*, about love being the only thing you can take with you when you die, is the essence of meaning, and especially poignant now that Patrick has passed. In Barbara Walters' second famous interview of Patrick, on January 7, 2009 (which was the last interview Patrick did), she brought up the subject. She asked Patrick if he ever thought about his movie, *Ghost*, about the spirit always going on. Patrick answered that he thought about it often and it had a great deal of meaning for him.

Thus, Patrick always seemed to be on a quest for meaning and spirituality in life, and this is reflected in many of the film roles that he chose to play. When Patrick became ill with pancreatic cancer, his focus on meaning and spirituality became even stronger. It had always been very important to Patrick to make a difference in the world, with one way being to use his craft to give people enjoyment, meaning, and richness. Way back in 1988, Patrick had talked to Barbara Walters in her ABC interview about wanting to use his work to make people's lives lighter. Patrick told Gavin Esler in the BBC *HARDtalk Extra* interview in 2006:

**I've always had the desire to be something, to accomplish something, to count for something. I have to have a sense of passion and purpose in my life or the little bird dies inside of me. And I think it's all of our jobs to keep that little bird of innocence alive and to keep the cynicism out 'cause the world wants to make us all very, very cynical and destroy everything that is worth believing in. Even movies now are starting to attack our faith.**

I think, once again, when he was diagnosed with pancreatic cancer, knowing that he made a difference in the world and was going to leave a meaningful legacy became even more important for Patrick. Hopefully the outpouring of support and love from multitudes of people, including professional colleagues and fans, Patrick received during his illness cemented in his mind and heart that he had touched millions of people's lives through his work and his spirit.

The sheer quality, diversity, and volume of Patrick's work, including thirty-three cinema movies, four television movies, seven Broadway shows, and numerous television appearances and roles, I think really speaks to his awesome talent, work ethic, spirituality, and ultimately his dream to make a difference in the world. The diversity, in just movie roles alone, included playing a dancer in *Dirty Dancing* and *One Last Dance*, to a drag queen in *To Wong Foo, Thanks for Everything! Julie Newmar*, to a pedophile in *Donnie Darko*, to a hockey player in *Youngblood*, to an attorney in *Jump!*, and on and on.

I ponder all of the attempts to recreate Patrick's movie roles into movie and television remakes and stage productions, such as:

1. *Dirty Dancing* was turned into a very successful international stage show (minus Patrick's song "She's Like the Wind") and into a three-hour television musical (seemingly replacing an aborted attempt at a movie remake).

2. *Ghost* was turned into a musical.

3. *Red Dawn* was turned into a movie remake.

4. *Point Break* was turned into a movie remake and into *Point Break Live*, a live comedy show (referred to as the first "reality play") with a member of the audience selected to perform Keanu Reeve's role, Johnny Utah.

5. *Road House* was turned into a movie remake.

This remake situation is sort of a two-edged sword in that it can be looked at as a rip-off and/or disrespect to Patrick, or as a tribute to the awesome work Patrick did in these movies. One thing is for sure, none of these remakes will ever have the same quality as the ones Patrick performed in because there simply is no one who can come close to his performances. Upon Patrick's passing, his *Dirty Dancing* co-star, Jennifer Grey, called him "an original." Kenny Ortega, choreographer of *Dirty Dancing*, told the *Hollywood Reporter* in 2011 that Patrick created the standard for men dancing in the movies for his generation.

Andrew Dansby, from the *Houston Chronicle*, wrote shortly after Patrick died:

**Like John Travolta, the Houston-born-and-raised Swayze was an entertainer ahead of the times and behind them. He was an old-school performer, a trained dancer who turned to acting but remained unafraid to break into dance on film. He bridged a lengthy gap between the golden era of Hollywood musicals and *High School Musical*.**

Alex Simon said in "Great Conversations: Patrick Swayze" on June 10, 2015:

From his screen debut in *Skatetown, USA* in 1979, to his final appearance on television's "The Beast" as a take-no-prisoner's cop, Swayze was an unapologetic good ol' boy who happened to be a classically-trained dancer, student of martial arts and Eastern philosophy, and possessor of an IQ that was nothing to sneeze at.

Carrie Rickey, *Philadelphia Inquirer* film critic, from the Jessie Baker NPR show said on September 15, 2009: "Swayze's Dancing Brought Characters to Life":

> There's a moment where he kind of leaps off the stage where he's dancing with Jennifer Grey into the audience, and I heard a gasp, a collective gasp from the audience. It was like watching Baryshnikov crossed with James Dean.

Of course, I must mention that true to Patrick's mother's way of insisting that her students be diverse in the arts, Patrick was also, in addition to all of the above-mentioned, a singer and composer. Elliott Sharp comments in an April 2013 article "Patrick Swayze-The Lost Tapes" in Noisey.com:

> Everybody knows we lost a wonderful actor when we lost Patrick Swayze. . . . The one thing about Swayze that hasn't been fully addressed is how much he loved music. That's an understatement: Swayze didn't just love music, he made music. He was a singer and a songwriter.

Patrick was offered recording contracts at a young age and sang and played guitar at coffeehouses during the early lean years. By 1987, Patrick had made a recording studio at his ranch. In 1989, Patrick spoke about not wanting to commercialize his music. He talked about getting into his music more in the 2000s. I personally heard him talk about this dream at the *One Last Dance* premiere in 2003 at the champagne reception following the screening of the film. He also spoke about this goal in the Official Patrick Swayze International Fan

Club Interview in London on November 27, 2005, and while ill with cancer, he mentioned that he was working on new music.

Patrick's most famous song was "She's Like the Wind," which was co-written by Patrick and Stacy Widelitz, and performed by Patrick, featuring Wendy Fraser. This song was originally written for the 1984 movie *Grandview USA,* and went on to become, as we all know, one of the most popular songs in *Dirty Dancing.* The inspiration for the song was Patrick's wife, Lisa Niemi. The hit reached #3 on *Billboard* Hot 100 and #1 on *Billboard* Hot Adult Contemporary in 1989. Also, in 1989, the song won the BMI (Broadcast Music, Inc.) Film & TV award for The Most Performed Song from a Film. The BMI reported that "She's Like the Wind" had officially charted its four millionth public performance in April 2009.

Regarding Patrick's other songs, "Cliff's Edge," composed and sung by Patrick, was used in *Road House* and Patrick also performed "Raising Heaven (in Hell) Tonight" in that same movie. "Brothers" written by Patrick and performed by Patrick and Larry Gatlin, played in *Next of Kin.* "Finding My Way Back" and "When You Dance" were in Patrick and Lisa's 2003 *One Last Dance* movie. "Finding My Way Back" was composed by Patrick, David Mc Vittie, and Allegra Day, and performed by Patrick. "When You Dance" (my personal favorite song by Patrick) was composed by Patrick, Erich Bulling, David Mc Vittie, and Allegra Day, and performed by Patrick, featuring Suzie Rose and Jimmy Demers.

In the 2006 *The Fox and the Hound 2* (video), Patrick was a performer in the songs "We're in Harmony" and "Hound Dude." Patrick and Larry Gatlin performed the song "Love Hurts" in Roy Orbison's honor at the Roy Orbison Tribute Concert, which was a fundraiser for the homeless in 1990. If that wasn't enough, Patrick also gave a touching speech at the tribute concert and then joined in with multiple stars in the ensemble performance of "Only the Lonely."

As a side note, Patrick also appeared as a dancer in Toto's 1982 music video "Roseanna" (along with Cynthia Rhodes who co-starred with him later on in *Dirty Dancing*) and as an actor in Ja Rule's 2002 music video "Reign."

Also, Elliott Sharp comments on the connection between Patrick and rappers after the release of the movie *Ghost*, in terms of them using "Swayze" in their lyrics, instead of "I'm ghost," which meant "I'm leaving," "I'm out of here." Rappers who have used "Swayze" in their songs include Kool G Rap, Method Man, Dres, The Notorious B.I.G., PMD, and Young Jeezy.

Speaking of ghost references, the 2016 remake of the movie *Ghostbusters* includes dialogue about Patrick and *Ghost* and several of his other movies, including *Road House, Dirty Dancing,* and *Point Break*. So this is yet another example of Patrick's work that has become a permanent part of our culture.

Getting back to Patrick and his music, Elliott Sharp makes an interesting assertion that there must be more songs recorded by Patrick than those mentioned above.

**We'd be fools to believe that these are Swayze's only songs. There must be more. He loved composing and singing way too much to have recorded only six tunes. Nobody only records six tunes. He must have left tracks chilling in an archive somewhere, waiting to be discovered, waiting to be shared. Maybe they're raw, lo-fi, bedroom four-track recordings. Maybe they're fully formed, hi-fi, studio hits. No matter what the songs sound like, I want to hear them. And I'm not the only one. Until these lost tapes are made public, the specter of Swayze is haunting us.**

It sure would be nice to hear more music by Patrick. One can only dream.

And speaking of dreams, I think that Patrick starring in the 2003 *One Last Dance* with Lisa and George De la Pena fulfilled a dream of many of his fans, which was to see Patrick dance again on the big screen. Dance was just such a big part of Patrick's life; one might say that dance was at the core of Patrick's soul. So even though Patrick had stopped dancing professionally years before *One Last Dance* was made, it was still so big of a part of who he was. Thus, dealing with not dancing anymore professionally was part of the reason for making the play, which was eventually made into the movie. Once again, Patrick spent his childhood and teen years dancing, including performing in many, many musicals in high school, performing with the Houston Jazz Ballet Company and the Buffalo Ballet, going on tour with Disney on Parade, and eventually training and dancing in New York with the Harkness Ballet School, the Joffrey Ballet Company, and the Eliot Feld Ballet Company.

Patrick, Lisa, and Nicholas Gunn had written and put on a play *Without a Word* at the Beverly Hills playhouse in 1984, which won six LA Drama Critic Awards. *Without a Word* was so popular and touched so many people's hearts that there were many requests for it to be turned into a movie. For around twenty years, Patrick and Lisa worked to make that happen and they persevered and accomplished their dream with *One Last Dance* being released in 2003, with Lisa as the writer, director, producer, and star, and Patrick as a producer, star, and financier. *One Last Dance* tells the story of the concert dance world from the perspective of dancers (semi-autobiographical) and how it is never too late to realize one's dreams. There are stunning dance sequences with Patrick and Lisa. The score is wonderful, and as mentioned earlier, there are two songs that Patrick sings that were also written by Patrick (with co-writers).

Patrick and Lisa did around five years of prep work to get back into dance concert shape for *One Last Dance* and took around three years to do the choreography for the movie. They used four chore-ographers for the film: Alonzo King, Dwight Rhoden, Patsy Swayze, and Doug Varone. Patrick's sister, Bambi Swayze, performed as one of the dancers.

I had the very good fortune of attending the premiere of *One Last Dance* at the WorldFest-Houston International Film Festival in 2003 and attending a screening of the movie at the Nashville Film Festival in 2004. It was so clear by watching Patrick and Lisa introduce the film (in Houston) and speak about the film (in Nashville), by talking to Patrick briefly (in Houston and Nashville), and then of course viewing the film (on DVD) many, many times, that dancing was one of Patrick's biggest passions, if not *the* biggest.

Patrick spoke about *One Last Dance* (which they had just been to Slovakia to promote) to the *Boston Globe's* Mark Shanahan in a September 29, 2005 interview:

**Everywhere we take this film, people want something to make them feel good. Hope is a big thing.**

In the same interview, he was also asked why audiences respond so strongly to dance. He replied:

**The world loves dance. It's our first form of worship. It's primal. Moving to rhythm is a powerful thing that's innate in all of us.**

Furthermore, I personally heard Patrick speak about the importance of dance, and all of the arts, twice at the Music Hall in Detroit (2002 and 2004) during his introduction speech for Complexions Contemporary Ballet. After each performance, Patrick hosted a gala reception that raised money for Complexions. Patrick served on the Complexions Board of Directors, along with Lisa, for this extraordinary, ethnically diverse dance troupe. Complexions is comprised of dancers from all over the world who not only perform innovative concerts all over the globe, but who offer dance workshops to inner-city kids.

In both of Patrick's speeches, he emphasized how important the arts are and how the arts distinguish us humans from beasts. He spoke about how important it is to get the kids away from the TV and computer, and get them involved in dance and the arts before it is too late. He remarked in the 2002 speech that dance could unite the world. In the 2004 speech, Patrick talked about how dance is an opportunity to communicate in a unique way. In addition, in 2004, Patrick focused on how kids today aren't growing up with the same opportunities or support regarding having and reaching dreams. He stated that we have to make it our job to support the dreams of children. He referenced the book *The Little Prince* where grown-ups were referred to as "given-ups." He talked about how he is a hopeless romantic and wondered previously if there was a place for him in the world. He said that he discovered that there were other people out there who were also hopeless romantics, but it was covered up.

I cannot say enough about how thrilling it was for me twice to be sitting in the first row (of course not the best place to see a dance concert) listening to Patrick give the introduction to Complexions and then having the opportunity to meet Patrick at the gala reception at the Detroit Athletic Club immediately following the performance. It made it even more special to watch *One Last Dance* at the Houston and Nashville screenings and at home on my DVD, having seen Complexions perform live, as they were the dancers in *One Last Dance*. Mr. Dwight Rhoden, Artistic Director, Co-Founder (with Mr. Desmond Richardson in 1994), and resident Choreographer at Complexions, of course, was in Detroit for the events. He created *Mercy*, a two-part ballet dedicated to Patrick after he passed. *Mercy* premiered at the Joyce Theater in New York in 2009.

By the way, working with family members on *One Last Dance* was not the first time in his career that Patrick worked side-by-side with family. Throughout the years, Patrick and various family members collaborated, including Patsy assisting Patrick with the 1979 Pabst Blue Ribbon beer commercial; Patrick and Lisa starring in *Steel Dawn* in 1987 as Nomad and Kasha respectively, shot in Africa; and Patrick and his brother Don Swayze both appearing in Patrick's last movie, *Powder Blue* (released in 2009, shot in Los Angeles in 2007). In *Powder Blue*, Patrick played Velvet Larry, a sleazy owner of a strip club, and Don played a bouncer. Of course, I have to mention *Swayze Dancing*, the 1988 dance instructional video featuring Patsy, Patrick,

Lisa, and Bambi, which was choreographed, written, and directed by Patsy (with Marc Lemkin as co-director). The dance performed by Patrick and Lisa at the World Music Awards in 1994 is so beautiful and still viewed and enjoyed by so many people. Patsy helped Patrick develop his razzle-dazzle number (the big dance in which Patrick does soft-shoe surrounded by beautiful women) as Billy Flynn in the 2003–2004 *Chicago*.

Finally, Lisa directed "My Brother's Keeper," the eleventh episode of Patrick's 2009 television thirteen-episode series, *The Beast*, in which he starred as a veteran FBI Agent, Charles Barker. Don was in Chicago to help support Patrick while *The Beast* was being shot.

As a side note, Patrick and Don were proudly at their mother's side and introduced Patsy, when Patsy was given the Ruth Denney Award for Lifetime Achievement at the Tommy Tune Awards in May 2004. Patrick spoke about Patsy to Greg Hernandez in an *Orange Coast* magazine interview in July 2004:

**For so many years, she has choreographed and nurtured young talent, Swayze says. She seems to give people that belief in themselves against all odds to move on with their life.**

Former students of Patsy include: Debbie Allen, Randy Quaid, Jaclyn Smith, and Tommy Tune. Debbie Allen spoke to newscaster Robin Roberts in a 2009 interview about how Patsy took her into her Houston dance school as a child, and how due to segregation, this was not even allowed at the time.

When Patrick received his star on the Hollywood Walk of Fame on his forty-fifth birthday on August 18, 1997, the photos show a very proud Patrick and, of course, very proud family members: his wife, his mother, his two brothers, and his sister. Coincidentally, *Dirty Dancing* was also re-released on this date, which was ten years after the original release. At the ceremony when Patrick received his star on the Hollywood Walk of Fame, he thanked everyone. He spoke about how much this honor meant to him and how this was only the beginning of his career.

Speaking of awards and Patrick's influence on other actors, I would like to begin with a very famous example of how Patrick's actions influenced Whoopi Goldberg. She has said many times that if it were not for Patrick, she would not have her Oscar for her performance as Oda Mae Brown in *Ghost*. From thanking Patrick during her Oscar acceptance speech at the Academy Awards, to speaking about it in various interviews and on *The View*, she recounted how Patrick fought for her to get that role. As an interesting note, Patrick appeared as a guest actor on her live television show *Whoopi* in 2004 on the episode "The Last Dance." Of course, Patrick danced with Whoopi on the show.

Natalie Portman has said in interviews that *Dirty Dancing* was a huge inspiration for her career and the movie she has seen the most. In a *Movieline* interview by Don Roos (*Love and Other Impossible Pursuits* filmmaker) on September 17, 2009, she was asked to discuss her favorite scene from *Dirty Dancing*. First, she spoke about how sad she was about Patrick Swayze passing. Then she discussed that her favorite *Dirty Dancing* scene was when Baby talks to her dad about how she is working on coming into her own and how she is sorry if she disappointed him.

Also, in regards to his influence on other actors, I think that throughout Patrick's career, in addition to being a very intense actor, he also used his energy and playfulness to help create a good ambience on the set. By doing so, this of course resulted in a good outcome and ultimately contributed to Patrick realizing his dreams and helping others realize their dreams. Patrick was known to sometimes be a prankster on the set, illustrated by this excerpt from the Official Patrick Swayze International Fan Club 2000 interview of Jordan Brady, director of the 2002 film *Waking Up in Reno*, in which Patrick played Roy Kirkendall:

**OFC: Are there any amusing incidents/pranks played, or**

stories from the filming that involved Patrick and that you'd like to share with us?

JB: Patrick was always and I mean always keeping the energy and humor up on set. But on one particularly stressful day, an hour after he was wrapped, Patrick rode up to set on his electric scooter, wearing a bathrobe, a long redneck wig and buck teeth. He circled the crew a few times and then disappeared. His timing was perfect! We all had a laugh and were recharged to finish our work.

OFC: Is your word 'law' on the set as Director, or would you ever take suggestions from experienced movie actors such as Patrick?

JB: Patrick was a tremendous ally. He understands story and structure inside and out. He always knew where 'Roy' was emotionally, which helps when shooting out of order. Moviegoers will always be able to pick up the subtleties of his characters. And Patrick is also tapped into what an audience needs from a story. . . .

OFC: We know Patrick has a good sense of humour and he showed a talent for comedy in *To Wong Foo* . . . Does *Waking Up in Reno* develop this talent?

JB: To me, Patrick has always played the Big Hero. In *Reno* his character is second fiddle to 'Lonnie Earl' for most of the film. If you read the script, you would rightfully assume that Swayze was going to play 'Lonnie Earl'—and he could have—too easily. But instead, Patrick plays 'Roy' naïve and sweet, dim-witted not dumb, and gets some of the biggest laughs in the movie. I also encouraged ad-libbing, since Patrick, a Texan, grew up with these types of people folks.

**Most of Roy's asides and good ole boy phrases in the film are Patrick's ad-libs or stuff we'd come up with together on the fly.**

Patrick was known to get along well with the other actors, the crews, and the people who worked behind the scenes in his movies. Sam Elliott, co-star in *Road House*, told Will Harris in a 2013 Random Roles A.V.Club interview that even more striking about Patrick than his physical talent was that he was a gentleman. Jake Gyllenhaal spoke in a 2017 interview to ET Online about how supportive and kind Patrick was to him during the filming of *Donnie Darko*.

It is reported that Patrick had a close relationship with Om Puri, co-star from *City of Joy*. In fact, Patrick wrote the foreword of the 2009 biography *Unlikely Hero: Om Puri*, penned by wife Nandita C. Puri.

When I spoke on January 8, 2017 to Scott Wilder, stuntman in *Point Break, The Renegades, and Black Dog* about working with Patrick, he said:

**He was an incredible, tough guy with amazing athletic abilities. . . . He was just a great guy and a friend.**

During my April 22, 2012 interview of Tom and Patt Rocks, husband and wife, who were dance extras from the *Dirty Dancing* Lake Lure set, Patt shared her thoughts on working with Patrick during the filming of the movie:

**He was very nice to the extras.**

**I had a chance to talk to him. He's a nice guy. I admire him. But when he danced, I couldn't catch my breath. I really couldn't. He was just a fabulous dancer.**

I asked the Rocks how many times Patrick jumped off of the stage while practicing the last scene.

**TOM: I didn't keep count, but it was a number of times. What would you say, Patt?**

**PATT:** No more than half a dozen.

**TOM:** Six, eight times.

**PATT:** He could jump because he studied at the Joffrey Ballet in New York after he left his mother's studio. At the time, remember Patrick was thirty-five years old. When he would jump off, I couldn't even catch my breath–when he would do that, and he landed on his knee and did a twirl. When the camera stopped, he would just almost collapse in pain.

Here is an anecdote from my March 2009 interview of Mike Porterfield, who worked as the lead line cook during the shooting of *Dirty Dancing* at Mountain Lake Hotel in Virginia and who currently is the head chef there:

**I'll tell you about Buddy. He came in the kitchen one night to get his beers. We had a dishwasher who had just recently gotten out of the Marines. This was a really weird little guy. The only way we could get him to work was to let him drink wine. He brought his own wine. We didn't provide it. We let him drink it 'cause he would stay there and work. It was Maddog or Red Lady 21—one of those fortified wines. Buddy came back in there and was talking with him. He asked him, "Do you want a drink of beer?" and he said, "Sure," and had a big pull on the bottle. We just got a big kick out of that. Buddy was a really down-to-earth guy. He was not in the least bit pretentious. He would invite us out to the library to have beers with him.**

In conclusion regarding Patrick's career, I will use Patrick's words from the November 27, 2005 interview in London that he gave to the Official Patrick Swayze International Fan Club:

**It's not the history making movies that is the reason I've had a thirty-year career—it's much longer than a thirty-year**

career when you think I came out of the womb on the stage! I've always had an uncanny knack whether it's a small movie or not, to find those characters, to find those roles even if they are dark characters to leave you out on the other end, that's changed in some way or seeing things in another way or some level of identification that gets people to look from a different point of view. Usually I like it to be something that has to do with heart.

I've just always had a sense of what the world wants. Right now with this surface, shallow world of reality TV and everything worth believing in being devalued or laughed at, or if you have integrity "What's wrong with you?" I'll never stop living my life by those clichés. You know, "Only the strong survive," "Nobody said it would be easy," "Back up your mouth" and "Give all you can because it will be returned." What I'm getting at is the cult following movies from *Road House* to *Point Break* to *The Outsiders*, now *Three Wishes* and *City of Joy* and now *Tall Tale* is picking up more people.

And of course, Patrick spoke often about how grateful he was for the wonderful successes of *Dirty Dancing* and *Ghost*.

Credit: SNAP/REX/Shutterstock.

*Patrick Swayze as Johnny Castle and Jennifer Grey as Baby Houseman in the iconic finale dance scene of* Dirty Dancing. *Their eyes reflect their heart and soul connection.*

Credit: Paramount/Kobal/REX/Shutterstock.

*Demi Moore as Molly Jensen and Patrick Swayze as Sam Wheat in the famous* Ghost *romantic pottery wheel scene.*

Credit: Tom Sanders/Aerial Focus.

*Patrick Swayze skydiving as Bodhi during the filming of* Point Break *over Perris Valley Drop Zone.*

Used with permission of Joshua Sinclair.

*Patrick Swayze as Richard Pressburger in the 2008 Joshua Sinclair film* Jump! *The true story of the acclaimed celebrity photographer Philippe Halsman is told with a focus on his murder trial in 1928 in Austria. Patrick plays the attorney who helps Philippe Halsman fight against the rampant anti-Semitism of the time.*

## CHAPTER THREE

## MORE ABOUT PATRICK'S ROLES

Patrick often played heroes who championed specific causes in his performances, which supported his desire to use his work to make a difference in the world. Once again, he used his sensitivity, acting skills, spirituality, and work ethic to create these diverse, memorable heroes. From the many, many examples of his hero characterizations, I have chosen four of Patrick's roles to focus on: Jed Eckert in *Red Dawn*, Vida Boheme in *To Wong Foo, Thanks for Everything! Julie Newmar*, Richard Pressburger in *Jump!* and Charles Barker in *The Beast*.

### Red Dawn

Patrick played Jed Eckert in the 1984 *Red Dawn* in which he is the leader of a group of young people who wage guerilla warfare on the enemy, the Soviet Union, who has invaded the United States. Here is an excerpt about *Red Dawn* from the September 1984 interview of Patrick by Joe Leydon, Houston film critic:

> **He [Patrick] knows the new film, which has opened to great box-office but lousy reviews, has been perceived as bloodthirsty, right-wing rabble-rousing. But he sees an anti-war message in the film—that, he says, is why he played the role of a teen-age freedom fighter who battles Red Army invaders in Colorado.**

### To Wong Foo, Thanks for Everything! Julie Newmar

Taking another look at *To Wong Foo, Thanks for Everything! Julie Newmar*, Patrick also speaks to Joe Leydon in September 1995 about realizing how being a drag queen is very courageous and how he worked it out emotionally to get the role of Vida Boheme right.

Swayze says, "I began to see that to make a choice in your life to be a drag queen is a very, very courageous thing. Because what you're doing, potentially, is alienating everyone you love in your life. And that takes a lot of courage. But all of a sudden, it also hit me: What a healthy point of view to come from if this is who you are. Because it's making a very conscious, specific choice to not be buried in your past and your pain, and not wallow in it. It's a choice to make your present be different, so that you'll have the hope of happiness in your future. And that's when I *got* Vida. I just went to the Elia Kazan point of view, which is, your character is revealed by how you conceal the emotion. Not by how you play it or wear it on your sleeve. That's not what we do as human beings. We go to our last breath trying to look OK, to try to look fine. Vida for me was the personification of that. Even to the level of trying to fix everybody else's life. It's only to try to make herself feel better, to like herself, to have a sense of self-worth. Sure, her pain's there. But you don't need to play that. I needed to play her nurturing qualities. So that's what I started doing. I looked at all the parts of Vida that hopefully exist in all of us. The compassion, the loving, the nurturing. That's when she started coming together for me."

Patrick told Greg Hernandez, in an *Orange Coast* magazine July 2004 interview about his performance as Vida Boheme:

It was my opportunity to create a character who was truly an angel, Swayze says. But I thought playing a drag queen was a big ol' lark, and I'd play a big old queen. But in rehearsal when I play-acted it, it didn't work. I realized her job was to be the heart of this movie.

[Miss Vida] stands for every drag queen on the planet or for anyone who has been misunderstood. It turned out to be the most emotional thing in my entire career, and I'm pretty proud of it, he says.

## *Jump!*

The third role that I am going to highlight is Patrick's characterization of Richard Pressburger, attorney for Philippe Halsman, in the 2008 Joshua Sinclair film *Jump!* From the *Jump!* press kit, used with permission of Joshua Sinclair, Writer, Director, Producer, and the exact wording therein:

A true story. The dramatic experiences of the young, later world-famous photographer, PHILIPPE HALSMAN in Austria in the '30s are the base of this exciting movie. *JUMP* shows the viewer abysses and tells of love, hope and future at the same time. Abysses of an unexpressed love between father and son, that eventually leads to a crash. Abysses of a politically influenced justice system, that leads to the conviction of an innocent human being. And *JUMP* is about the righteous, which are obsessed by their beliefs.

### *SYNOPSIS*

September 10, 1928: An accident occurs at the Tyrolean Zillertal that leads to a spectacular circumstantial evidence lawsuit that causes a stir far beyond the Austrian borders. The Jewish dentist Morduch Halsman (Heinz Hoenig) whose origins are in Riga/Latvia goes on a mountain hike with his 22 year old son Philipe (Ben Silverstone). Morduch Halsman dies during this journey. His son's version of the story: His father fell. Philippe Halsman is arrested due to patricide suspicions. His lawyer (Patrick Swayze) is able to get a reprieve for the misdemeanant with help from prominent intercessors like Sigmund Freud, Albert Einstein and Thomas Mann. Halsman later escapes to New York. He makes photos for over a hundred covers of the *LIFE* magazine. With his portraits of Marilyn Monroe, Richard Nixon and many other prominent people of his time, he becomes world famous. Halsman's 'Jump photos' are still legendary today.

*THE SCRIPT*

Writer and director Joshua Sinclair read the court documents and press articles in Innsbruck from this time and talked to family members of Halsman, before writing this story. Director Joshua Sinclair about *JUMP*: "Nobody, no matter what color or race, should be pre-judged. Unfortunately this happens every day worldwide, even 80 years after the Halsman case."

*Excerpt from THE STORY*

Philippe's mother and sister succeed in finding a lawyer in spite of the fast-growing anti-Jewish movement. The lawyer Richard Pressburger (Patrick Swayze), who is also Jewish, becomes his lawyer.

Thus, Patrick plays a real hero, Richard Pressburger in *Jump!* Per Mr. Sinclair, Pressburger was a real person and also:

We do not know for sure, but I believe he did die in a camp because he stayed in Austria too long trying to save Jews.

On May 16, 2009, Patrick was awarded Best International Actor for his portrayal of Richard Pressburger.

## The Beast

Finally, the last role I am going to feature is Charles Barker, the unorthodox FBI agent, in the television dramatic series *The Beast*. Jan Griffith wrote a moving essay on one of the episodes of *The Beast*, which illustrates Patrick's wonderful acting skills, his uncanny knack to capture the essence and heart of a character, and his ability to bring a poignant focus to an important issue: veterans.

## The Best of *The Beast*

## By Jan Griffith

*Featured in the August 2009 Official Patrick Swayze International Fan Club Magazine.*

My favorite episode of *The Beast* was "Mercy." (If you haven't seen it, you may want to watch it first. I've tried not to give away too much here.) The story was current—veterans were being killed. Barker and Dove are assigned to find out who is murdering American soldiers. They both end up going undercover to get their man.

Why do I think this was one of the best episodes? One, we got to see both Barker and Dove face some of their demons from their past military service, which made for a great story within the story. (Besides, Travis is really great looking in a military uniform.) Two, it is also the first time that Dove discovers something of Barker's past, and I think realizes that Barker is a "good guy" and not a rogue agent. Finally, I think Patrick gave one of his best performances ever in this episode. Throughout the episode Patrick seamlessly switches between being Barker and a homeless veteran. In a breath he goes from tough FBI agent to a quiet man struggling to find his place at home.

There were three scenes or sequences that really stood out for me. Patrick's (or rather Barker's) first night at the homeless shelter when he is confronted by the manager and then protects the people there was truly touching—he sounds just like a soldier with his polite "yes, sirs" and got lots of details right. He jumps when there is a loud crash off camera. (Former soldiers typically react to loud noises even years after they return home.) Second, there was a scene between Barker and another female veteran talking in a car about her experiences in Iraq and how slow the government is to respond to veterans' needs.

Patrick's humor and gentle nature came through so well. Finally, at the climatic ending, Barker faces the psychiatrist that has been killing veterans, and Patrick's monologue about having to kill a young boy with a piece of blue curtain was moving and powerful. Patrick struck the perfect balance of emotion—anger, fear, sadness, and regret were all there. The scene was done almost entirely in close up on Patrick's face, and he portrayed each emotion powerfully, but in an understated, real way, mostly with his eyes.

After that emotionally charged speech, he changes into Barker in a second with his no-nonsense way of working and his dry humor—directed at Dove. But the real twist? Dove asks Barker if the story he'd just told was true, and Barker responds, "Did you believe it?" Dove says he did, to which Barker responds with a smirk and a dry, "Then I did my job." As the episode closes though, we see Barker in the dark holding a reminder of his story, a piece of blue curtain—it was true after all.

This episode touched me deeply. Like many people, I have relatives who served our country bravely. Sometimes we forget that even though our soldiers may return home to us—many have wounds that we cannot see. This episode brought that issue to light, as well as showing a very human side to Barker. I truly hoped that Patrick would be acknowledged for this episode. It says a lot about him as an actor, how good he really is. Though he has never served in the military, his performance shows great compassion and understanding of those who have. So BRAVO, Patrick!

Courtesy of Betty Rollins.

*Patrick Swayze walking his dog at the* Dirty Dancing *North Carolina film location.*

Courtesy of Betty Rollins.

*Patrick Swayze and extras, including Betty Rollins, in the ballroom at the* Dirty Dancing *North Carolina film location.*

Credit: Moviestore/REX/Shutterstock.

*Patrick Swayze as Dalton, a Zen bar bouncer,* in Road House.

Credit: Moviestore/REX/Shutterstock.

*Patrick as Max Lowe, a disillusioned doctor, in* City of Joy.

Credit: Moviestore/REX/Shutterstock.

*Patrick Swayze as a beloved drag queen, Vida Boheme,
in* To Wong Foo, Thanks for Everything! Julie Newmar.

Credit: Rhyser/Kobal/REX/Shutterstock.

*Patrick Swayze as Jack McCloud, a spiritual drifter, in* Three Wishes.

## *JUMP!* GALLERY OF PHOTOS

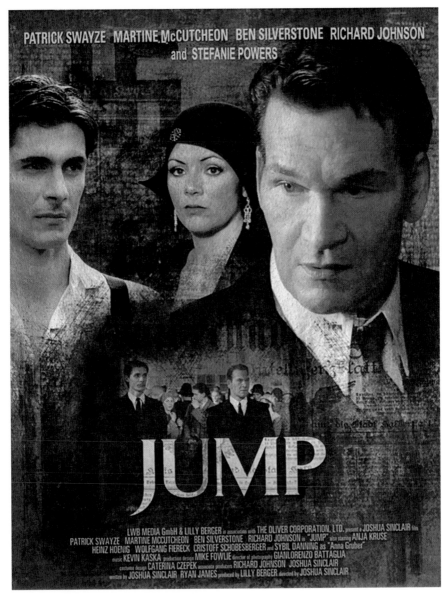

Used with permission of Joshua Sinclair.

Jump! *poster for the 2008 Joshua Sinclair film for which Patrick Swayze was awarded Best International Actor on May 16, 2009.*

Used with permission of Joshua Sinclair.

*Patrick Swayze in* Jump! *Just hired as the attorney, Richard Pressburger, to represent Philippe Halsman.*

Used with permission of Joshua Sinclair.

*Patrick Swayze, as Richard Pressburger, preparing his case in* Jump! *while traveling by train with Philippe Halsman's mother and sister.*

Used with permission of Joshua Sinclair.

*Patrick Swayze working on his case as attorney, Richard Pressburger, with his private investigator in* Jump!

Used with permission of Joshua Sinclair.

*Patrick Swayze, as attorney Richard Pressburger, getting ready for court with his private investigator in* Jump!

Used with permission of Joshua Sinclair.

*Patrick Swayze in court as the attorney for Philippe Halsman in* Jump!

Used with permission of Joshua Sinclair.

*Patrick Swayze (Richard Pressburger) in* Jump! *outside of the courtroom near the end of the trial where he had just been looking out of the window at the extensive Nazi activity.*

Used with permission of Joshua Sinclair.

*Patrick Swayze as Richard Pressburger receiving the verdict in* Jump!

Credit: Fitzroy Barrett/Globe Photos, Inc.

*Patrick Swayze receiving his star on the Hollywood Walk of Fame on August 18, 1997 (his birthday), flanked by his mother, Patsy Swayze (left) and his wife, Lisa Niemi (right). Back row from left, Don Swayze and Sean Swayze, his brothers, and his sister, Bambi Swayze.*

CHAPTER FOUR

# LOVE:
## Marriage and Family

Patrick is well known for having been a romantic and a guy who wore his heart on his sleeve—which was like his father. As mentioned in chapter two, Patrick himself stated in a 2004 speech at the Detroit Music Hall, in which he introduced Complexions Contemporary Ballet, that he was a "hopeless romantic." While performing in Disney on Parade at around age twenty, he played Prince Charming and even back then believed in true everlasting love, such as in the fairy tale of Prince Charming and Snow White.

Patrick married Lisa Niemi on June 12, 1975. They had met in 1971 at Patrick's mother's dance school (where both were students) when Patrick was nineteen and Lisa fifteen. They were known to have one of the longest-lasting marriages in Hollywood. In the July 2004 interview to Greg Hernandez, *Orange Coast* magazine, Patrick spoke about his marriage:

> **Relationships are hard, but you never give up, Swayze says. You go through phases. We always try and remember that you have to keep falling in love over and over again and discovering new things about each other.**

When Patrick was very ill from the cancer, Patrick and Lisa renewed their wedding vows in the summer of 2008. It was a ceremony held in front of a few close people.

For Patrick, there was that crossover between dreams in real life and dreams in performances regarding love. Patrick often spoke about love being a connection with the eyes and soul.

Some of Patrick's most romantic roles were: Orry Main in *North and South*, Johnny Castle in *Dirty Dancing*, Dalton in *Road House*, Sam Wheat in *Ghost*, Jack McCloud in *Three Wishes*, and Travis MacPhearson in *One Last Dance*. In interviews, Patrick talked about how awkward filming sexual scenes could be and how he focused on the emotional connection with his partner, rather than "the bumping and grinding" to make the scenes as good as possible.

As a side note, Patrick's reaction to being named the "Sexiest Person Alive" in 1991 by *PEOPLE* magazine was typical Patrick. He did not wish that he had not received this accolade and he did appreciate it, but at the same time, he took it all with a grain of salt. I find it endearing that he was the honoree of all of the Sexiest Men Alive awardees who wrote the introduction for the *PEOPLE* special issue "20 Years of the Sexiest Man Alive." In a November 29, 2005 article in the *Daily Mail* by Lester Middlehurst, Patrick is quoted as saying:

> **That's not to say that being voted the world's sexiest man doesn't make you feel king for a day, but I don't think I'm God's gift to women or some kind of walking aphrodisiac.**

In a November 25, 2005 interview by Xav Judd published in 6degreesfilm.com regarding the 2005 movie *Keeping Mum*, Patrick elaborated on this topic:

> **Q: Were you attracted to the idea of sending up your heart-throb image with *Keeping Mum*?**

> **A: I love taking the piss out of myself. It was like the Saturday Night Live that I did. I'm really cautious about not allowing my ego to rear its ugly head. The moment you buy the hype, the moment you buy "the sexiest man alive" stuff I think it's over with. *Keeping Mum* was part of that process of giving me a chance to make fun of myself.**

Back in 1991, Patrick's mother, Patsy, was quoted in *PEOPLE* as saying that Patrick did not think he should be considered an idol—that he just thought of himself as a regular Texas kid.

It is very obvious that Patrick valued his family immensely and looked out for them. He was very close to his father, mother, and four siblings: Vicky, Don, Sean, and Bambi. His father had the nickname Buddy, and Patrick was called Little Buddy initially, and then throughout the later years after Patrick's father died, Patrick was known as Buddy. Patrick spoke to the *Daily Mail* in the November 29, 2005 interview about his father:

**He was a gentle soul, an incredibly intelligent man who could do the *New York Times* crossword in 15 minutes. My mother was the driven one, while he wore his heart on his sleeve. I took after my father.**

Strikingly, both Patrick and his father died at the age of fifty-seven. It is well known that Patrick had a very hard time dealing with his father's sudden death from a heart attack in 1982, including that his drinking became a problem at this point in time. Also, Patrick assumed much of the responsibility for the family. A positive way that Patrick chose to cope with his father's death was to set the goals of owning a horse ranch to honor his father and to make his father proud of him for the rest of his life. These dreams of Patrick did come true in spades.

When Patrick was struggling with his illness of pancreatic cancer, he seemed to find comfort in knowing that his father was on the other side. It appeared that he used his spirituality to get through this difficult time, including trying to have his angels guide him, which of course included his father.

An absolutely devastating loss for Patrick and Lisa was Lisa's miscarriage in February 1990. Even though it is reported that later on they had considered adoption, they never had children.

When Patrick's older sister, Vicky, committed suicide in 1994 at age forty-five, this was another devastating loss for Patrick. The November 29, 2005 *Daily Mail* article quotes Patrick:

> **Her death changed my life, says Swayze. It was hard not to feel responsible, that I could have done something to prevent it. The longer your life goes on, the more death you face. After my father, my manager, and then my sister died, I started to feel like I was cursed.**
>
> **I had to find something to believe in, outside of myself, to beat the guilt and blame I felt—particularly in Vicky's case. Suicide is not something I am capable of, but there are a lot of people out there who kill themselves because life can take you to some hard places and not everybody can cope with that.**
>
> **The only thing you can do in those circumstances is to find some kind of meaning. You have to take that moment and make a promise to yourself that you will honour the spirit of the person you have lost for as long as you live. I have made my life better so Vicky's death doesn't seem quite so pointless.**

So once again, it seems that Patrick took an adverse situation and worked to take something from it and make it positive.

Patrick's mother, Patsy, died on September 16, 2013, at age eighty-six, which was only two days later in the same month, September, when Patrick died.

*Patrick Swayze at the Complexions gala in 2002 at the Music Hall in Detroit with a dance intern. Sandy Duncan, Music Hall board member, is observing.*

## CHAPTER FIVE

## DANCE:
## Patrick's Dreams for Himself and Others

Patrick definitely had a dream to advocate for the arts, and espe-cially for dance. In the course of working on achieving his dream about dance, he helped make dreams come true for a multitude of dancers.

First of all, Patrick was obviously a role model for aspiring male dancers. Patrick proved that a male could still be masculine and a dancer. Following the success of *Dirty Dancing*, there was an explo-sion of people signing up for dance classes; both men and women, and a whole new generation of male professional dancers who were influenced by Patrick's performance as Johnny Castle. These male dancers include Tatum Channing, Joseph Brown, and Paul-Michael Jones (the latter two starred in the stage production of *Dirty Dancing*).

I did a 2012 interview of Jackie Horner, consummate dance professional and story consultant to *Dirty Dancing*, who continues, to this day, to give lectures about *Dirty Dancing* and dance lessons (which include dance steps from *Dirty Dancing*) in the Catskills. She commented on the continuing influence of the movie on dance:

> **And, you know, it [*Dirty Dancing*] has helped tremendously the dance business. It really has, and continues to. Twenty-five years later, you still have people say: "I want to learn this," or, "I want to do that." And we have *Dancing with the Stars*, *So You Think You Can Dance*, and all these wonderful things that come on. I think basically because of that.**

By the way, Patrick did not view *Dirty Dancing* to be his dance film. He told Joe Leydon, Houston film critic, in August 1987:

**But, you know, I don't consider *Dirty Dancing* to be my dance film. Because Johnny Castle is from the streets of South Philadelphia, you know. So he's not a virtuoso . . . It was frustrating, but also very interesting, in creating character, and resisting my own ego. Because I'm a much better dancer than Johnny Castle. Yet to be true to the character, and try to make the character come to life, I had to make him from Arthur Murray's. He was pretty good, for a street kid. And good enough for exhibition ballroom kind of stuff. But not as a truly trained dancer.**

Patrick definitely considered *One Last Dance* his dance movie. By the time *One Last Dance* was filmed in 2001, Patrick was much older (age forty-nine) and had to make some adjustments in his dancing to accommodate his body. However, as mentioned previously, Patrick got back into amazing concert dance shape and did awesome dancing in the film.

In the Official Patrick Swayze International Fan Club Interview, Part 2 conducted in London on November 27, 2005, Patrick spoke about how *One Last Dance* had become a catalyst for promoting dance and the arts. He first talked about what an honor it was to have the Joyce Theater Gala fundraiser centered on *One Last Dance*. At the time, it was hoped that the Joyce Theater would be part of the development of the Twin Towers site in New York where so many people died in the tragedy of 9/11 in the year 2001.

**After we finished the major push for *One Last Dance* after 20 years, then this incredible event that we did at the Joyce Theater that was a phenomenal Honour and opportunity for the Gala performance and fundraiser to be centered around *One Last Dance* and all our dancers. . . .**

We've really turned into the spokespeople for the Dance World and the Arts World and we're doing tons of speeches. We've just finished launching the first Dance Festival on the West Coast in Laguna Beach, we just did an event for Dancers for AIDS and it was all based on the future stars of tomorrow; these young dancers and young dance companies, so we are getting the opportunity to go out there a lot with the Nevada Ballet and we can turn this into a life's work. . . .

Everyone wants us to do the same format that we did in the Joyce Theater—live dancers and then use their local dancers and with the film and benefit screenings, because it can bring in lots and lots of money to the Arts. It's something we really, as much or more than Conservation, we have a passion about, which is our artistic sensibilities and our creative abilities and passions are the only things that separate us from the beasts and make us special.

When you look at the United States, the United States are systematically eliminating artistic classes for kids! It's insanity. We're going to build generations of computers, soul-less computers. People don't realise that nurturing that side of ourselves, nurturing that compassion, and that ephemeral and keeping that little bird alive and the child alive, which is the only way that we resist cynicism and becoming jaded. Those are the things that nurture our passion about preservation, conservation, everything. It's like the basis of where the goodness in us began and the hope continues.

In Patrick's quest to promote dance in all ways possible, he supported the reality television show *Dancing with the Stars*. In 2005, the first season of *DWTS*, he made a guest appearance per E! Online. He also provided some coaching to one of the contestants John O'Hurley and was there in the audience for the finale. *DWTS* did a tribute show dedicated to Patrick after he passed.

Patrick did a cameo role as a dance instructor in *Dirty Dancing: Havana Nights*, which was a prequel to *Dirty Dancing* and released in 2004. One only wished that he had played a bigger role. The movie obviously did nowhere as well as the first and one and only, original *Dirty Dancing*.

Looking at significant roles Patrick did as a performer in musical stage shows, he was a dancer and servant in the Broadway 1975 *Goodtime Charlie* production in which Joel Grey (Jennifer Grey's father) played the lead role. It was while performing in *Goodtime Charlie* that Patrick met Jennifer Grey, who was fifteen, for the first time. Patrick starred as Danny Zuko in the original Broadway production of *Grease*, which helped open the door to go on to success in movies and television—as afterwards he debuted in his first movie role as Ace in *Skatetown, U.S.A.* in 1979 and played in his first television role as Pvt. Gary Sturgis (a soldier with leukemia) on *M*A*S*H* in 1981. He played Billy Flynn from 2003–January 2004 in the Broadway production of *Chicago*. Finally, Patrick performed as Nathan Detroit in *Guys and Dolls* at the West End in London from July 27–December 2, 2006.

An interesting fact is that when Patrick was starring in *Guys and Dolls* in London, the stage show of *Dirty Dancing* was playing across the street. Also, when Patrick was shooting his television series *The Beast* in Chicago, the stage show of *Dirty Dancing* was playing there. Patrick told an amusing story to the *Chicago Tribune* about another coincidence. He said that one day while filming *The Beast* and crossing the street as his character, Barker, he saw two cabs with ads for *Dirty Dancing* go by.

Patrick posthumously received the Rolex Dance Award on November 2, 2009 at the twenty-fourth anniversary jubilee of Career Transition for Dancers at New York City Center.

Credit: Roger Karnbad-Michelson/Globe Photos.

*Patrick Swayze, 1988, with one of his horses, Cloud.*

## CHAPTER SIX

## CONSERVATION:
### Patrick's Dreams for Himself and Others

With Patrick's upbringing and heritage from his father's side of the family to be close to the land and to horses, and to treasure the cowboy life, it is no surprise that he was into conservation. Patrick bought his five-acre ranch in the San Gabriel Mountains, eventually named Rancho Bizarro, in 1984, after acquiring his starring role as Orry Main in *North and South*. Owning the ranch was a tribute to his father, which was one of Patrick's dreams. It also afforded the chance for him to get back to nature and the cowboy life, and served as a haven from Hollywood. The property bordered the Angeles National Forest. Patrick and Lisa took advantage of the opportunity to ride into the forest and commune with nature whenever they could. Patrick and Lisa had various animals on the ranch, including horses, dogs, cats, and peacocks. They began their dream of owning, working with, and showing Arabian horses during this time.

In the late 1990s, Patrick bought his New Mexico ranch, which consisted of almost fifteen thousand acres of land, and once again Patrick and Lisa spent as much time as they could at the ranch, riding and camping. Patrick did a tremendous amount of conservation work on his New Mexico ranch, which he talked about in the November 27, 2005 London interview to the Official Patrick Swayze International Fan Club:

**I now have ten years of the product of what I've done (on the Ranch). I have thinning I did at the two year point, the four,**

five and six year point. So now you can drive through my Ranch and see the results. Not going in to seriously clearing out all the crap, but just getting rid of the diseased and the unhealthy stuff first and then getting out some of the spindly stuff so all the trees are not fighting for the water so much.

I can tell you that I have a stand of trees that I thinned eight years ago and they were that big around (he gestured about three inches) and they are now big (he showed they are around 14 inches!). I've realised that I can create old growth forests in my lifetime! You have to understand what I am trying to do is—I spent a lot of money to get a specialist to come in and help me plan a two hundred year forest stewardship plan. I plan on doing a two hundred year plan in twenty years. It's happening! You are now able to drive through my forests and see the examples of what I'm doing and the potential for it. The hard part is there is no market for this type of timber. They only (the companies) want big millable timber.

But I've now found markets for it. With one company that is getting ready to move on to my property, with all their machinery that goes in and grooms the forest, recreates it all, reseeds it as they go. Within two years you will never know anything had been done there! I've now found markets—all of Mexico's construction and architecture is based on "latillas" timber. Then the firewood market and if it comes off, I may pull off a deal—because what you do with all the little stuff that's left is you grind it up and mulch it.

Patrick's horsemanship and love of animals helped get him lead roles in *North and South* (1985), *Tall Tale* (1995), and *King Solomon's Mines* (2004). On June 6, 2004, Karl J. Paloucek (Source: *Channel Guide Magazine*) interviewed Patrick about his role as Allan Quatermain in the soon-to-be premiere of the Hallmark channel's adaptation of *King Solomon's Mines*.

> I feel it's completely and totally who I am, he says. For me, doing Quatermain was like coming home. . . . I live this kind of life. I live on a horse [ranch] in the mountains. I raise Egyptian Arabian horses and cattle in the timber farm; I'm a wildlife [preservationist]; I'm a battler of poachers. It was quite interesting for me.

> Paloucek: The film, shot on location in South Africa, is beautiful to look at, alive with arresting landscapes and exotic animal life.

While filming *King Solomon's Mines* in Africa, Patrick became even more inspired to work on conservation and preservation of wildlife. He even, for a while, explored the idea of a conservationist reality TV show.

In a September 24, 2009 article in *Mother Nature*, "Patrick Swayze remembered for conservation efforts" by Katy Rank Lev, it is noted:

> He also heavily supported the Galinas River Watershed Restoration Plan, donating large sums to help the U.S. Army Corps of Engineers in conjunction with the New Mexico Environment Department to preserve the land near his property. In 2005, Swayze helped to successfully relocate the Galinas River, which had veered from its original course, and, according to the River Restoration Action Plan, vastly improved the habitat for fish and wildlife.

Credit: Sony TV/Kobal/REX/Shutterstock.

*Patrick as rogue FBI Agent Charles Barker in the 2009 television show*, The Beast.

CHAPTER SEVEN

# CANCER:
## Patrick's Dreams for Himself and Others

Patrick made a surprise appearance opening the Stand Up To Cancer television fundraising broadcast at the Kodak Theater on September 5, 2008. He received a standing ovation when he took the stage. He spoke eloquently and from his heart, asking people to stand up to cancer with him. He said he was dreaming of a future that included a long and healthy life. This show was a milestone event as it was sponsored by ABC, CBS, and NBC and broadcast to more than fifty countries. There were a ton of celebrities on the telethon. One of the founders of Stand Up To Cancer, Laura Ziskin, a renowned film producer (which included being executive producer of the 2008 and 2010 Stand Up To Cancer shows), who herself was battling breast cancer, commented in a blog "Remembering Patrick Swayze and a Campaign to End Cancer" on November 16, 2009:

> For all the star power that night—the stunning musical collaborations, the participation of the presidential candidates and the profiles of breakthrough scientists, Patrick stole the show. He was the living embodiment of what it meant to bravely "stand up to cancer" . . . In the year that followed, Patrick continued fighting, not just for his own life, but on behalf of the more than 35,000 people who die from pancreatic cancer every year and the 1,500 people who die from cancer every day.

Stand Up To Cancer was founded in 2008 by Laura Ziskin and eight other women in the entertainment industry who were affected by cancer. It is a program of the Entertainment Industry Foundation that focuses on acceleration of development of new therapies by utilizing teams of the brightest cancer researchers to do collaborative, innovative cancer research. Goals of the organization include providing awareness, educating about prevention, and assisting more people diagnosed with cancer to become long-term survivors.

Sadly, Laura Ziskin died from breast cancer on June 12, 2011. Her work continues to make an impact on cancer research and treatment via the ongoing work of Stand Up To Cancer, including specific endowments she left to Stand Up To Cancer.

The next television appearance of Patrick was the ABC Barbara Walters interview "The Truth" that aired on January 7, 2009, that was filmed at Patrick's California ranch in December 2008. This show was an hour that consisted of Patrick baring his soul about his fight against pancreatic cancer. He shared his feelings and his ways of coping with the cancer in the typical Patrick way, by being real. The tough questions were asked by Barbara Walters and answered by Patrick and Lisa. I think that this was another huge way that Patrick had an impact on a multitude of other people with cancer and their families, and to really everyone, by serving as an inspiration in the way he was battling the cancer with tenacity and grace, and living his life as fully as possible. Patrick's life at this point included of course doing his new television show *The Beast*, going camping, working/being with his horses, and more.

I really think it was very brave on Patrick's part to do the Barbara Walters show. The show was his chance to tell people what he wanted them to know. I can tell you that the guestbook for his official fan club (for which I was one of the people monitoring) actually crashed right after the show because there were so many people trying to get on it. Sadly, this was the last interview Patrick did.

Getting back to Patrick being an inspiration for how he dealt with his cancer, I just love the story that many people talked about, including Patrick (in his autobiography), Don, his brother, and Dr. George Fisher, his oncologist, as to how Patrick reacted when speaking to his oncologist after being given his diagnosis. The story goes that Patrick basically asked his doctor to show him and to explain the cancer to him so he could use that knowledge to mount an aggressive, proactive fight against it. Also, Patrick's positive, warrior attitude was reflected in a saying he created during his cancer battle: "Nobody puts Patrick's pancreas in a corner." Patrick was thus one of the bravest people I have ever met.

I think that one of the basic tenets that Patrick practiced in his life that he initially learned from his father as a teen was: *You never give up*. This principle had served Patrick well throughout his life in dealing with adversity, including dealing with his knee injury in high school that plagued him his whole life, and this came even more strongly into play in battling the cancer. The sheer determination and grit that Patrick displayed in his cancer battle was just so impressive. Whoopi Goldberg spoke on *The View* about Patrick's fight against cancer, right after he passed, saying that Patrick was someone who just never gave up.

Some people wondered why Patrick would work on a television show when given a terminal diagnosis. I think that the bottom line goes back to Patrick loving his craft and using that to keep a good outlook, wanting to be productive, and wanting to give something to the world. Patrick is quoted in the *New York Times* on October 28, 2008:

**How do you nurture a positive attitude when all the statistics say you're a dead man? Mr. Swayze asked. You go to work.**

*The Beast* pilot for this A&E television network series was shot in December 2007 (just prior to Patrick's cancer diagnosis in January 2008) and aired on January 15, 2009, followed by twelve more episodes. Patrick only missed one and a half days of shooting, which was reportedly from a cold. How he managed to put in the long thirteen-hour days on the set during the week and get his chemotherapy on the weekends was miraculous.

On February 8, 2009, the *Washington Post* ran an op-ed written by Patrick: "I'm Battling Cancer, How About Some Help, Congress?" In his factual and eloquent piece, Patrick asked Congress to vote for the maximum funding to allow the National Institutes of Health to fight cancer and other life-threatening illnesses and gave the reasons for his request. He made reference to his family's way of dealing with challenges: "Stop talking about it, and *do* something about it." He said that is how he felt about getting more money for cancer research.

Patrick passed from pancreatic cancer on September 14, 2009 at his California ranch with Lisa and Don at his side. He had been an unbelievable warrior against the cancer and survived longer than most people with that advanced stage of the illness. He became a real-life hero and an inspiration to millions of people. He never did give up and thus he did win that battle.

After Patrick died, Lisa established the Patrick Swayze Pancreas Cancer Research Fund at the Stanford Cancer Institute and became an activist for the Pancreatic Cancer Action Network.

The Prayer Circle for Patrick had been created in March 2008. Members included people from all over the world and from many different faiths and beliefs. By September 2009, the Prayer Circle for Patrick consisted of over 5,000 members.

The memorial for Patrick was held on October 4, 2009, on the Sony Studios lot in Culver City, California, where reportedly around three hundred mourners attended. Patrick's stallion, Roh, was there with Patrick's cowboy boots facing backwards in the stirrups, which is an old cowboy tradition.

Credit: Rick Smith/ Used with permission of the Music Hall Center for the Performing Arts.

*Una Jackman, Patrick Swayze, Maggie Allesee (Music Hall board member), two unidentified attendees, and Dwight Rhoden (Director, Complexions) enjoying the 2002 Complexions gala event at the Detroit Athletic Club.*

## CHAPTER EIGHT

# MY CONNECTION TO PATRICK, MY DREAM OF MEETING PATRICK, AND MY CHANNELING OF PATRICK

It all started for me when I viewed the May 11, 1988 Barbara Walters interview of Patrick Swayze after I had seen *Dirty Dancing* countless times. Previously, in 1985, I had seen parts of *North and South*, the television miniseries in which Patrick played one of the lead characters, Orry Main. At the risk of committing blasphemy, I did not really become engaged with the show and it did not have that much of an impact on me. However, watching *Dirty Dancing* was a totally different story. The movie really resonated with me right from the first time that I saw it. I started going to see it in different movie theaters and sometimes I would even go in midway through the screening. I loved that the movie had heart, wonderful dancing and music, and a happy ending to a true love story. I was enthralled with Patrick Swayze's sizzling, sensitive, and romantic portrayal of Johnny Castle.

I was in a tough spot at that time in my life, as I had just had a break-up with the man I thought was my soul mate. Viewing *Dirty Dancing* was a wonderful escape and took me out of my heartbreak into a new world of hope. I was definitely more than a little intrigued with Patrick Swayze. Then when I saw the 1988 Barbara Walters interview of Patrick at his California ranch, it hooked me into becoming not only a bigger fan of Patrick, the actor, but also of Patrick, the person. I was stunned by how genuine, down-to-earth, introspective, passionate, and sensitive Patrick was during the show.

In particular, when he spoke about honoring his father and about wanting his work as an artist to make people's lives lighter, this really moved me. It was obvious that Patrick was not only a very talented (and of course good-looking) artist, but he also was a man who did a lot of soul searching, who valued family, who was gracious, and who wanted to make a difference in the world, and this really struck a chord in me. So after watching the interview, I made it a point to see all of Patrick's work and tried to learn all that I could about Patrick from other interviews and articles written about him. The more I did these activities, the greater my connection to Patrick became.

I made contact with the US fan club in 1987 and was sent an auto-graphed picture of Patrick by the club (which of course I still have). When online in 2000, I discovered the Official Patrick Swayze Inter-national Fan Club, and of course I joined. The fan club president, Margaret Howden from Scotland, was very welcoming. I began to receive quarterly magazines and photos. I had never had this type of connection with a movie star or celebrity, and I certainly had never joined a fan club until then. I relaxed regarding my concern about this sort of "adolescent" behavior when I realized that I was not the only person having some kind of special connection with Patrick. Soon, joining the club and becoming part of the Patrick community was really rewarding, interesting, and fun.

A friend of mine told me that I was going to meet Patrick one day and I told her that was crazy. Then, actually, in 2002, I met Patrick for the first time (which would eventually total four times) right here in Detroit, as he appeared with Complexions Contemporary Ballet to introduce their concert and to host a gala fundraiser for them. Patrick and Lisa served on the board of directors for Complexions. I had no idea what to expect about meeting Patrick at the Complex-ions event. It was really striking and helpful to me that Margaret called me from Scotland to prep me for my upcoming meeting up with Patrick. She told me that this was highly unusual for Patrick to host an event like this and provide photo opportunities for fans. She assured me as to how down-to-earth Patrick was and that everything was going to go well. I was not disappointed to say the least. I sat in the front row of the concert venue, the Music Hall in Detroit, with my Aunt Nedra, who graciously took me to the event. I really liked what Patrick spoke about in his introduction of the dance troupe (as I reported in chapter four), about the importance of engaging children and teenagers in the arts, and overall the importance of the arts in all of our lives.

After the dance concert, I was certainly not the only person anticipating Patrick's appearance and meeting Patrick at the gala at the Detroit Athletic Club being hosted by him. I could just feel the excitement and electricity in the air while everyone was waiting for Patrick. The Complexions dance troupe had already come in and people were milling around at the refreshment tables. Finally, Patrick entered the hall and made a speech and then danced with various people and signed autographs and gave photos for everyone. It really was a wonderful night for me as I did get to personally meet Patrick and of course get his autograph and a photo. I was a little let down as we were trying to hold a conversation, but Patrick could hardly hear me as we were pretty close to the band. I experienced Patrick's attention to his fans and his Texas manners when my aunt had difficulty getting the flash on my throwaway camera to work. Patrick took the camera from her and waved it in the air and asked for someone to take our picture, and someone did.

I ended up meeting Patrick three more times: in 2003 at the Houston World-Fest International Film Festival for the premiere of *One Last Dance*; in 2003 at the Nashville Film Festival at a screening of *One Last Dance*; and in 2004 in Detroit once again for another Complexions concert and fundraiser gala. Each experience was unique and very special.

My experience in Houston was life-changing for me because it inspired me to pursue my dream of being a writer, as well as having this wonderful feeling that I could realize other dreams as well, and that people were basically good. In addition, by spending some time at the film festival with Patrick, mostly as part of a group (although there was also a one-on-one interaction between me and Patrick in which we discussed the Complexions event in Detroit), and viewing *One Last Dance*, I felt like I had gotten to know Patrick as a person a little bit. This experience confirmed for me that he was a very good man, just as I had thought.

First, regarding being a writer, I had written numerous articles for the fan club magazine and found that really rewarding, but after being in Houston, I made a decision to expand my writing. I was very inspired by watching how proud and passionate Lisa and Patrick were about accomplishing their dream of making this movie—how they stuck with this project for about twenty years, worked so hard, and succeeded in making such a brilliant dance movie. And of course, as life imitates art or vice versa, the theme of *One Last Dance* was that it's never too late to realize your dreams. After spending time with Patrick and Lisa at the festival with many other fan club members (who had traveled from all over the world to attend the festival) and also meeting Patrick's mother, Patsy, and Lisa's mother, Karin, it really made one of my dreams come true. I will be forever grateful that I had that wonderful opportunity. In spite of discovering that I was sitting next to an air marshal on my flight home after the weekend (as this was post-9/11), I was still in a blissful state and feeling like I could accomplish many of my dreams.

Among other highlights of the Houston trip, I will always remember the very special surprise experience of Patrick and Patsy coming on the fan club's tour bus in Houston and allowing us to ask them questions for almost an hour. (Please see a detailed account of this experience in chapter eleven.) It was really wonderful to watch the banter back and forth between them and the obvious loving, close relationship they had. I was really struck by how humble and fun Patrick was throughout the weekend and how he took time to interact with all of the fans at the champagne reception following the movie. I would guess that there were around one thousand people in attendance. I watched Patrick racing around the reception area, with minimal security, to meet every fan. He treated every person with respect and graciousness, whether the person was young or old, good-looking or not, disabled or not. He even took to rolling around on the floor with the Seeing Eye dog of one of the fans. I heard Patrick speak to a group of fans about his dreams for his music. It was just totally surreal. I am so grateful that I was actually able to purchase a video of the reception. I honestly do not think I could watch it now because it would be too bittersweet, but I know it is there if I am ever ready.

In Nashville, I attended another screening of *One Last Dance* with two wonderful fan club members, Jan Griffith and Shirley Penrod. We also went to the Q&A with Patrick, Lisa, and Stacy Widelitz (composer) regarding *One Last Dance*. Then when we met up with Patrick and Lisa at BB King's, a jazz club, that evening, we received the red carpet treatment. Each of us had the opportunity to speak to Patrick one-on-one and then had a group photo taken on each of our cameras. As we were saying goodbye to Patrick, he humbly thanked us for coming to the festival and supporting the movie. Just when I thought, *Okay time to go*, Patrick leaned over and gave me a big hug and did the same for the other two fans. This experience, once again, confirmed that Patrick was one of the good ones.

At the second Complexions event in Detroit in 2004, Patrick again, when introducing Complexions, spoke about the importance of the arts. I had another opportunity to speak with him and some of the Complexions staff and to see the wonderful Complexions company dance.

I did have the chance, while on a pre-planned family trip to visit my family in California, in January 2004, to go to San Diego and see Patrick as Billy Flynn in *Chicago*. It was very exciting to see Patrick on stage. He looked mighty dapper and I could just tell that he was so enjoying himself while giving that performance. A very unusual occurrence happened after the show that afternoon: Patrick did not come out the back-stage door to greet his fans. Security told us that Patrick needed to rest and get ready for the evening performance. It turned out that Patrick had actually been ill during his performance (which he told me when I spoke with him in Nashville). As we all know, the show must always go on!

Regarding another Patrick experience, I did have the opportunity to be one of three fans who called in a question to Patrick during his appearance on May 25, 2005, on the CNBC television show, *The Big Idea with Donny Deutsch*. It was really cool to have the experience of being involved in the taping of the show. I was actually sitting in my bedroom on the telephone waiting for my turn to speak and got to hear all that was going on in the background. I think I sort of sounded like a dork at first when it was my turn, but I did, in my opinion, come up with a really good question for Patrick. I also think Patrick really liked my question and took it very seriously. Patrick had not been informed ahead of time that fans would be calling in questions. My question and Patrick's answer actually became the foundation for this book and they can be found in the closing chapter of the book.

In late 2005, I was chosen "Obsessive of the Month" by *LOOK/ Entertainment Weekly* magazine regarding my interest in Patrick. A photo and short story about my enchantment with Patrick was published in the magazine.

On December 23, 2012, on the way to pay a very special visit to my dad in California, I had the good fortune to visit Madame Tussauds Hollywood Wax Museum to see Patrick's wax figure. It was a really bittersweet and profound experience for me to view Patrick's wax statue as the character Johnny Castle in *Dirty Dancing*. As I wrote in my last book, I felt overcome with emotion and thought: *If only Patrick were really still here*. I could only speculate that somehow Patrick knew about his statue and enjoyed it. This balancing on-the-log scene was a really wonderful choice from *Dirty Dancing* because Patrick is surrounded by trees and nature—which he loved—and is doing what he loved: meeting a challenge and utilizing his natural dancing/athletic grace and ability. I did take the opportunity to enjoy this tribute to Patrick and to say what I wanted to say to Patrick. I thanked him for all that he was still doing for me by his portrayal of the character Johnny Castle and most important, by the way he lived his life with boundless passion, spirit, courage, and dignity, which serves as great inspiration to me.

In closing, in addition to giving me motivation and hope to achieve some of my dreams, I have channeled Patrick in various other ways. I would say that his practice of never giving up and fighting for what he believed in and for his health has influenced me greatly. In fighting my own health battles, I have been able to stay on the path largely because of inspiration I derived from Patrick. In trying to stand up for what I think is right, even though it may sometimes be unpopular and cause consequences, once again, I look at Patrick's examples of him standing up. Finally, Patrick's search for meaning in life and his fighting his demons have resonated with me and provided motivation to me in my pursuits. The whole point of Patrick being inspirational to me in these various ways is not that Patrick was perfect without faults, but that he was a down-to-earth, genuine guy who shared his struggles and did so with courage, grace, and humility, especially while battling cancer. As I said in my writing years ago, Patrick played many heroes in his artistic work, but he became a real-life hero to me while "fighting the enemy" in the last part of his life.

Taken inside of Madame Tussauds Hollywood. Image shown depicts wax figure created and owned by Madame Tussauds.

*Me and Patrick Swayze's wax figure during my awesome visit to Madame Tussauds Hollywood on December 23, 2012.*

## CHAPTER NINE

# MORE WAYS PATRICK MADE DREAMS COME TRUE FOR OTHERS

Patrick told Donny Deutsch on the CNBC *The Big Idea with Donny Deutsch* show on May 25, 2005:

**I love seeing if I can make dreams come true for other people.**

Patrick was well known for treating his fans very well. He spent time with his fans at various events and kept them posted regarding his work projects and appearances via the Official Patrick Swayze International Fan Club. During his appearances at events, he tried to give as many autographs and photos as he possibly could. I remember being in Nashville at the film festival and Patrick had just finished the Q&A. He was signing autographs. His security was trying to get him to leave and he just kept on signing and speaking with the fans until everyone had gotten an autograph and had a word with him (including myself). During the reception following the premiere screening of *One Last Dance*, Patrick was just amazing as he made a point of speaking personally to everyone in attendance, which was probably about a thousand people.

In his 2004 movie, *George and the Dragon* (filmed in Belgium), Patrick gave the opportunity for fan club members to be extras as nuns in the film. How thrilling was that for his fans!

As already mentioned in the previous chapter, three of us fans had the wonderful opportunity to ask Patrick a question on the May 2005 *The Big Idea with Donny Deutsch* television show. A producer had reached out to the fan club looking for interested participants and chose the participants based on the questions that were submitted.

When Patrick was playing Nathan Detroit in *Guys and Dolls* in London in 2006 from July 27–December 2, Patrick and Lisa met up with fans in a preplanned get-together, which was truly special to all of the fans who attended. Patrick was well known for coming outside the stage door of the Piccadilly Theatre to meet fans after the performance was over. Patrick made countless fans' dreams come true by being so available to shake their hands and speak with them.

Patrick spoke to entertainment reporter Greg Hernandez from *Orange Coast* magazine in July 2004 regarding appreciating his fans:

**Fans have been so faithful and been behind me for so long, he says. I'd like to believe it's because I never forget that fans are the people who put you where you are at. I really appreciate that, and I've been able to have a career that keeps going and going and going.**

Another way that Patrick helped make people's dreams come true was his involvement in the Arabian horse world. He was a wonderful horseman and role model/ambassador for the Arabian horse world. He participated in fundraisers for scholarships for youth riders, among other things.

Patrick was involved with many charities and causes. One of his appearances that caught a lot of attention was at the third annual Day of Dance for Heart Health on February 25, 2006, at Robert Wood Johnson University Hospital in New Jersey. He was a guest speaker and focused on prevention and treatment for women in regards to cardiac illness. According to an article written by Annie Reuter, who attended the event and spoke to Patrick, Patrick shared with the audience that his father had died from heart disease at a very young age, which resulted in Patrick taking on much of the responsibility of the family. Patrick also lost his grandmother to heart disease.

A story regarding Patrick's kindness and caring for others was told to me by a member of the international skydiving community. A horrible tragedy occurred on April 23, 1992, when a plane crash in Perris, California, killed seventeen of the twenty-two people on board a plane carrying members of the skydiving community during a training period for the world championship. The entire Canadian, Dutch, and one of two American teams perished. Patrick and his brother, Don, had done some skydiving at the Perris Drop Zone, including Patrick shooting a scene for *Point Break*, which was photographed by Tom Sanders (see photo at the end of chapter two and read Tom Sanders' tribute in chapter ten). The Perris Drop Zone is a hub to one of the nation's busiest and most popular skydiving areas. The punch line to this story is that Patrick donated a bunch of items for the auction that was held to help families of the deceased.

I would be remiss if I did not mention the famous United Kingdom YouTube couple incident. Patrick surprised the couple, Julia Boggio and James Derbyshire, on *The Oprah Winfrey Show* on November 6, 2007, by coming on stage and dancing with Julia Boggio. At that point, this couple's wedding video—which shows them doing the *Dirty Dancing* finale dance—had been seen by more than two million YouTube viewers. And there was also the surprise appearance by Patrick on the 2005 *Today Show* in which he said the famous *Dirty Dancing* line to a big fan: "Absolutely, nobody puts Donna in the corner," and then took Donna for quite a dance spin.

A special phenomenon that has occurred with Patrick's fans is that some of them developed close friendships with each other that continue to this day. Personally speaking, I can attest to this. I have some very special, treasured close friends and a circle of acquaintances because of the connection to Patrick. In addition, while researching and writing my three books, I have met so many people and had so many wonderful experiences and I attribute that, at least partially, to the Patrick connection.

Looking at a broader picture, and perhaps most important of all, I think that Patrick, by having been such a talented, kind, courageous, spiritual man, has provided a positive humanistic, spiritual energy that many, many people throughout the world tap into and expand. And in this day and age, that is a miracle in itself!

Used with permission of Joshua Sinclair.

*Patrick Swayze and Joshua Sinclair, Director, Writer, and Producer on the set of* Jump!

CHAPTER TEN

# TRIBUTES TO PATRICK

**From JOSHUA SINCLAIR, Writer, Director, Producer of *Jump!*:**
"Patrick fashioned his own life to conform with his spirituality and undying hope and resilience."

January 18, 2017

***"This is what I said at the LA Jewish Film Festival (2009) when we opened the Festival with JUMP! after Patrick's passing:***
I have been fortunate enough to work with many wonderful filmmakers in my career. Some you may have heard of, others not. But they are all exceptional and timeless in their art. Vittorio De Sica, Sofia Loren, Roberto Rossellini and young Isabella, Richard Burton, Romy Schneider, Richard Harris, Trevor Howard, Kim Novak, Marlene Dietrich, David Bowie, Sean Penn, Martin Sheen, Karen Allen, Grace Jones, and even Tony Curtis at the end of his Billy Wilder heyday. And I am not just name-dropping unless it is to drop this one name: Patrick Swayze. Patrick was Truth. The cowboy's need to survive at its purest. There was always palpable truth in his emotions even against the backdrop of Hollywood's lies, deceptions, hypocrisy and false myths. Patrick was and will remain forever a genuine myth because he represented the humanity inherent in show business distilled to its essence.

In all my career, I have never met such a dedicated and passionate human being—on and off the set. And that is refreshing to say the least. Patrick Swayze was that sort of miracle that comes along only once or twice in any given generation. It was my privilege to have loved him, to still love him now. Oscar Wilde once said: 'We are all in the sewer but some of us are looking at the stars.' Patrick was always looking at the stars, no matter what cards life had dealt him. And for that, I thank you Patrick—for your inspiration, for being a hymn to life. Some say we have lost Patrick. I say, no we haven't. I know exactly where he is."

**From JORDAN BRADY, Director, *Waking Up in Reno*:**

"Patrick was a dear man, extremely humble, and funny. Few reach his level of global fame as he did, and still stay so grounded."

September 18, 2016

**Excerpt from the 2000 Official Patrick Swayze International Fan Club interview of Jordan Brady about *Waking Up in Reno*:**

"Patrick was a tremendous ally. He understands story and structure inside and out. He always knew where Roy was emotionally, which helps when shooting out of order. Moviegoers will always be able to pick up the subtleties of his characters. And Patrick is also tapped into what an audience needs from a story. . . ."

**From ELEANOR BERGSTEIN, Writer, Co-Producer, *Dirty Dancing*:**

"People have said many fine things about Patrick when he was alive and in tributes later. All the fine things said were true. But I'm sorry I didn't speak up. I didn't want to intrude as the family and friends and fans gave all their most deserved accolades. But now I would like to say that Patrick was my loyal friend, my collaborator, from the moment I met him he was dear and close to my heart. But the thing that was singular and most impressive to me about him and needs saying again and again was that Patrick was a very good man. It was the thing that was most important to him, to be a fine and good man who spread kindness and honor wherever he went. He did do that—with his talent, his courage, his indefatigable desire to be the best he could for himself and bring out the best in others. With his beauty, his grace, and his generosity—it is this that I miss most about him."

April 1, 2017

**From LINDA GOTTLIEB, Producer, *Dirty Dancing*:**

"Patrick had a really good heart. If he liked you, you were his buddy, his friend. I saw him years later, and he gave me a very warm, loving embrace. He loved animals. Even when we were shooting, he was often on the phone checking about the animals. I think he was happiest back at his ranch."

November 17, 2012 (edited November 4, 2016)

**From PIPER LAURIE, Actress, *Tiger Warsaw*:**

"Patrick Swayze was perhaps the most intense, honest actor I've ever worked with. No horsing around, always prepared, and so earnestly wanting to be not just really good, but the best he could possibly be. He asked the director to ask me if I would mind shooting our first mother-son reunion scene without rehearsal. He wanted it to be raw and passionate. That was truly fine with me and it was a good choice. It turned into a very nice scene. I would have liked knowing him better. Gone much too soon."

January 10, 2017

**From MARSHALL R. TEAGUE, Actor, *Road House*:**

"Working with Patrick Swayze on *Road House* I had no idea at the time that I would end up with a friendship that transcended as strong as a brotherly love . . . In my acting career, I've had the pleasure of working with some incredible actors. Many of which I have developed wonderful friendships and bonds. Patrick and I connected on another level. We met as actors on the stage to engage in raw brutal combat; both sharing a martial arts, athletic background. As we rehearsed the fight scenes, we knew we could elevate the realistic intensity as we developed a choreography which turned the physical contact of this fight into a dance. End result, we created one of the best contact action fight scenes on film and a deep friendship for life.

Patrick was a special man, I miss him every day."

March 5, 2017

### From DIANE VENORA, Actress, *Three Wishes*:

"I had the chance to work with Patrick Swayze on *Three Wishes*. What I remember most about him was his real sensitivity toward the other actors, fierce professionalism, and FUN. All my respect to this wonderful actor and brilliant man."

November 2, 2016

### From SCOTT WILDER, Stuntman, *Point Break*:

"My main connection with Patrick was *Point Break*. In *Point Break*, Patrick had to surf and skydive. His brother [Don] was a master sky-diver. Don made Patrick comfortable with skydiving. Patrick talked all of the time about how he jumped with Don and how he just loved jumping. When Patrick jumped, he was just like a dancer in the air. Patrick couldn't wait to get off work and go to Perris, California (the skydiving capital of California) and jump.

I had to double him [Patrick] on the foot chase because he was out promoting *Ghost*.

With all of the stunts, he did everything. He was a great athlete. He was a great stuntman. He went above and beyond. One time, he hurt his knee earlier in the day. It had popped or something and he wanted to take down Keanu [Reeves] in the water. He did it and it was spectacular. That night, he had a doctor there to drain his knee. He was an incredible, tough guy with amazing athletic abilities. With all of his fights, he did beautiful. Patrick did all of his fights.

My father, Glenn Wilder, was a second unit director and stunt coordinator on *Point Break*. He really loved Patrick as well. Patrick was a definite blessing for the stunt coordinator and stuntmen.

He was a buddy.

He had been practicing surfing down south. We got him and brought him to Point Dume [Beach] and Little Dume [Beach] a few times to surf. One day, he slipped and fell down the trail into a trench. It was about a quarter of a mile to get to where we were going surfing. He realized that he lost his Rolex watch that his father had given him. About a month later, when we returned, Patrick found the watch. It was sweet.

The last time I worked with Patrick was on *Black Dog*. I did not have that much contact with Patrick. I did a lot of car stuff before the principal actors arrived. I also had worked with Patrick earlier on a couple of episodes on the TV series *The Renegades*.

He was an athlete, so he really loved his work. He was just a great guy and a friend. He was just like a brother. Any time, when I saw him, he was always cool."

January 8 and 27, 2017

## From TOM SANDERS, Stunt Skydiving Cameraman, *Point Break*:

"It is a BIG deal that Patrick trained and became a proficient skydiver to do some of the actual stunts involving skydiving. This is unheard of in Hollywood. I have been a SAG stunt skydiving cameraman for nearly 40 years and he is the ONLY one I recall doing his own stunts. They all say they do, but they don't. Patrick was a skydiver. He was the REAL DEAL in all aspects of life.

Regarding Patrick during the filming of *Point Break* over Perris Valley Drop Zone, Patrick called me up one day after the studio thought they had everything they needed. He asked me if I would come out to Perris, he would bring the 35mm movie film if I could bring the camera and make some jumps. Since this location did not match Lake Powell or California City where the two scenes were shot, I concentrated on up angle exit shots, track bys and deployments, but had to get one shot with the Perris scenery during the day. We didn't get paid, who would care, he just wanted, like me, to make the scenes as good as possible."

April 29 and 30, 2017

**From ALEX SIMON, Entertainment Journalist, Co-editor, The Hollywood Interview. Excerpt is from "Great Conversations: Patrick Swayze." June 10, 2015:**

"From the minute Patrick Swayze shook my hand, and for the next six hours we spent together, I was completely disarmed by his charm, honesty and just plain normalcy. After a half hour or so, I felt as though I was hanging out with a buddy from the old neighborhood (his Texas to my Arizona made us cultural cousins). Swayze was reflective, but totally un-self-indulgent. He was engaging, but usually more interested in your opinion than expressing his own. He was close to the earth as a rancher and man who loved the outdoors, yet also a man of letters who could put most PhDs to shame with his knowledge of, from what I could tell, almost everything. . . .

Goodbye, Patrick. Thank you for always staying down to Earth, even when Hollywood tried to cast you out among the stars."

## From JOE LEYDON, Film Critic
## Remembering Patrick Swayze at the HFCS Awards
## December 20, 2009

"*The Hurt Locker* and *Up in the Air* were the big winners Saturday when the Houston Film Critics Society announced the winners of its annual awards for excellence at the Museum of Fine Arts, Houston. But I kinda-sorta felt like I'd grabbed a big prize myself when I was selected to offer a tribute to the late Patrick Swayze, who was honored with this year's HFCS Lifetime Achievement Award. Just before the audience viewed a deeply moving montage (assembled by Jose Del Toro and Travis Leamons) of clips from Swayze's most memorable movie performances, I got to say:

I met Patrick Swayze for the first time back in 1983, when he dropped by the hotel where I was staying in L.A. that weekend to talk about his upcoming role in Francis Coppola's *The Outsiders*. It was supposed to be a brief chat, but it turned into a long, leisurely conversation. I remember thinking at the time this guy certainly seemed to have enough drive, determination and charisma to succeed in a very challenging field. I also remember being very envious of this guy, because when the valet finally brought around his car—it was a DeLorean.

I won't pretend that Patrick and I were close confidants or bowling buddies. But we did wind up talking several other times over the years. And we got to the point where I think we enjoyed each other's company—and even shared a couple private jokes. Right from the start, I noted his habit of describing how busy he might be at the moment, and how determined he was to get the next gig—and how he'd always end up shrugging, smiling, and saying: 'Hey, you work hard, and then you die.' Up until the very end, Patrick never stopped working—never stopped fighting. He struggled against expectations and preconceptions—and narrow-minded casting directors—to get cast against type in movies like *City of Joy* and *To Wong Foo, Thanks for*

*Everything! Julie Newmar*. And even though, ultimately, he lost that final battle we're all destined to lose, he fought the good fight long and hard with uncommon grace and inspiring dignity. But here's the thing: A man can die, but his movies are forever in the present tense. And I'm sure Patrick would be pleased to know that, even though he's left us, he's still with us. Because Patrick—with all due respect, wherever you are—you were only half right. If you work hard enough, you just might live forever."

Credit: Sue Tabashnik.

*Patrick's Hollywood Walk of Fame star, which he received on his 45th birthday on August 18, 1997.*

## CHAPTER ELEVEN

## SUE'S EXPERIENCE OF MEETING PATRICK

*This 2017 edited excerpt is from an article that I wrote for the Official Patrick Swayze International Fan Club magazine.*

### Second in a Lifetime Opportunity, April 20, 2003

I am writing to tell you that for the second time in six months, I had the opportunity to see and meet Patrick. And my second opportunity included meeting Lisa as well.

Initially, I saw Patrick on October 19, 2002, at the Complexions dance concert and afterglow in Detroit, Michigan. Patrick had introduced the Complexions dance troupe and then had hosted a benefit afterglow. I had been lucky and had my picture taken with Patrick at the October gala.

My second experience was that on April 4, 2003, I attended the 36th WorldFest-Houston International Film Festival 2003 to see the premiere of *One Last Dance* on opening night. Not only did I get another picture with Patrick and an autograph on the back of my October picture, I had the opportunity to talk to Patrick. Patrick and Lisa made themselves so available to their fans that it was unbelievable. In addition, Lisa's mother, Karin Niemi, and Patrick's mother, Patsy Swayze, made themselves accessible as well. I also received pictures and autographs from all of them on the *One Last Dance* poster. A big thank-you to Rosemarie [Ravenelle] for taking the picture of Patrick and me.

Highlights of the weekend in Houston for me included of course viewing the wonderful *One Last Dance* movie with fellow fan club members. It was very special to view the movie in reserved seats for the fan club right in front of Patrick's and Lisa's family and friends. Patrick and Lisa introduced the movie. I came away thinking: "Wow! Dreams can happen!" I do not think there was a dry eye in the theater during certain parts of the movie. When the movie was over, my first thought was: "I want to see this movie again—now!" I wondered: "Could it be the makings of another *Dirty Dancing* syndrome?"

I loved watching the dance scenes. The choreography and performances were unbelievable. I loved watching Bambi (Patrick's sister) dance. I enjoyed seeing again some of the dancers from Complexions who had performed in Detroit. I really got a kick out of watching the "older" dancers try to get back in shape, as I am in that age range also. I almost felt that I was right in the movie—it was so real! The movie contained humor, beauty, drama, love, heart, and two of Patrick's songs. What more could a person want?

Little did I know that the very next day, Patrick and his mother, Patsy would get on our tour bus and talk with us fans for about an hour. I had thought that maybe they would say goodbye and that would be it, but it was unbelievable that they spent so much time with us. I just so happened to be sitting in the second row, as my fellow fan club member, Rosemarie, had saved me a seat.

First, Patsy got on the bus and said that Patrick wants to talk to you. Then Patrick came on board and invited us to ask what we wanted to know. I loved watching the interaction between Patrick and Patsy. It was obvious that they have a special relationship. They answered questions including:

**Q: Fan: What was Patrick like as a child?**

**A: Patsy: Very confident. Always wanted to do everything. Always said he could do it (even if he couldn't do it) and would just go do it. . . .**

**Q: Fan: How did you meet Lisa?**

**A: Patrick: At the dance studio. Lisa had actually gotten lost, had been trying to find the acting class and went down the wrong hall and ended up in the dance studio. Lisa's wonderful dance physique was noticed right away. . . .**

**Q: Did you really hang off that truck in *Black Dog*?**

**A: Patrick: Yes.**

Patrick talked about how he did his own stunts. He said he had stuntmen do rehearsal takes, but he did the real take. The subject of Patrick's injuries came up, and it was said that actually he has had fewer injuries than would be expected considering the longevity of his career. Patrick talked about how he trained to deal with his injuries and how training has saved him.

Yes, I did get up the nerve to ask a question. I said that I had enjoyed *Three Wishes* very much and wondered why it didn't do better at the box office. Patrick answered that it depended on the studio, the timing, and so on. He talked about why that is the reason they are going through the back door with *One Last Dance*.

It was just great that Patrick and Patsy made time to spend with the fan club members, considering all that was going on and their busy schedules. They both were so gracious and genuine. I want to say a big thank-you to Patrick and Patsy.

Speaking of Patsy, I also very much enjoyed the several minutes I spent talking to her on Friday night towards the end of the champagne reception following the movie. I said to her:

**Maybe sometimes the fans get to be just too much?**
(I said this to her after hundreds of people had just succeeded in getting Patrick's autograph and/or picture.) She answered:

**Oh no. I am just very grateful.**

I had a chance to tell her how much I enjoy the Swayze dance video and she was so humble about it. Her accomplishments are just so awesome. Her Silver Foxes profile reports that she states her biggest achievement is being the mother of five children. The profile also describes her amazing career of being an award-winning chore-ographer and master-dance instructor for more than fifty years. Her choreography work includes the movies: *One Last Dance* (co-chore-ographer with Alonzo King, Dwight Rhoden, and Doug Varone), *Urban Cowboy, Thelma and Louise, Liar's Moon,* and *Hope Floats.* She was the founder and director of the Houston Jazz Ballet Company. She has gone to retirement homes and villages and done appearances to encourage people to be active and lead full, happy lives. In the A&E biography *Patrick Swayze All the Right Moves,* it is stated that Patsy has been Houston's premiere director and choreographer in opera, theater, and ballet . . .

Getting back to the Houston weekend, it was really great to spend time with the fan club members. I thought I knew a lot about Patrick, but I realized many of my fellow fan club members had more knowl-edge than I did and shared with me some information that was new to me.

I came away from the weekend very excited and happy, and an even bigger fan of Patrick. I reconfirmed my conviction that some sort of physical training is so valuable. I rekindled my belief that dreams can happen and that persistence and hard work will pay off. Also, I am reminded that if some people shut doors in your face, it is important to carry on with your beliefs and to follow your heart's dreams.

I would like to make special mention to Margaret for the wonderful job that she did planning, facilitating, and making the weekend so special. It was wonderful to be with Sandy, Thomas, and you. Thank you.

Once again, I give a big thank-you to Patrick and Lisa for a wonderful movie and to Patrick, Lisa, Karin, Patsy, Margaret, and the fan club members for making the weekend so special. *I had the time of my life!*

## CHAPTER TWELVE

## INTERVIEW OF A FAN:
## CATHERINE

Ireland, November 16, 2016 (email interview)

**What caused you to become a fan of Patrick?**

Patrick Swayze first came to my attention back in 1985 in the mini-series *North and South* as the incredibly handsome Orry Main. I was only sixteen at the time, but remember fondly watching this series on TV with my parents in its weekly installments. There was an amazing cast of Hollywood's most favorite actors in it, which really appealed to my parents of course. . . . James Stewart, Elizabeth Taylor, Jean Simmons, Johnny Cash, and more. However, my eyes were firmly fixed on this new guy I had never heard of before. He was jaw-dropping gorgeous and his name was Patrick Swayze. I was smitten forever! Oh, how I wanted to be Madeline. Orry Main is still my favorite of all Patrick's roles.

**Tell me about the Patrick Swayze Fan Club Facebook page that you run.**

**When did you start the page?**

**How many members do you have?**

**Where are the members from?**

**What made you decide to run the Patrick Swayze Fan Club page?**

There are many Facebook pages dedicated to Patrick's memory now, which I think is wonderful. After Patrick died there was still so much love for him worldwide that Facebook became the natural outlet for his fans to remember him.

I also wanted to join one of these pages, but I noticed that most of them were "public" profile pages and that put me off. I prefer a private page where fans can talk about their feelings for Patrick, have discussions, and share information about him and his work.

After searching for such a page, I came across the Patrick Swayze Fan Club page. There were four hundred members. It was fairly new and run by a Swedish lady. I was delighted to be able to join it and contribute. In fact, I contributed so much and so often that the lady in charge asked me to be an administrator with her for the page. I was more than happy to do this. As English was not her first language, she felt it would be good for the page that I could interact with members, who were mostly from English-speaking countries.

I have been administrator for the page for about two years now. My Swedish friend is still involved, but she has pretty much given the page over to me. We now have approximately 5,500 members from all over the world: Europe, Australia, and the United States. We welcome everyone who is willing to abide by Dalton's rule: "Be nice" from *Road House*. As administrator, I run the page by the same rule. I will: "Be nice, until it's time to not be nice." We are lucky to have some members on the page who knew Patrick personally, and it's always a treat to hear their stories and memories.

**Has Patrick helped you achieve any of your dreams, and if so, how?**

**How has Patrick inspired you and others?**

As I have already said, I became a fan of Patrick in 1985. Back then, of course, we didn't have the Internet to find out instantly everything we wanted to know about our favorite stars. So, for many years, I really didn't know much about him as a person, apart from the occasional magazine article here and there. I live in Ireland, so information on Patrick wasn't plentiful, but at least we did get his best movies in the cinema.

It's really only in the last few years that I have had the time and Internet access to be able to find out all about him. The more I learned about him, the more I liked and respected him. Being a Hollywood heartthrob and world-famous actor, it's easy to imagine that he would have lived a charmed life and be somewhat removed from the ordinary lives most of us live. Not so, as I quickly found out. His life was full of cruel twists and turns, which he faced head-on with a determination to succeed no matter what obstacles he had to overcome. A career in acting was never what he imagined for himself. Ballet and dance was his first love and very much what he wanted to do. How cruel then that despite being acknowledged as a rising star in the ballet world, his knee injury would end his ballet career prematurely. His ability to look beyond that and pursue other avenues for his creative talent says so much about him.

His never-ever-quit attitude is the reason he succeeded and became a famous actor. But no matter what Patrick decided to do in life, I feel he would have been the best at it. He never took on anything without giving 100 percent and more to it. He was a perfectionist and it shows in his work. He had a thirst for knowledge and was always excited to learn new things and experience different cultures in his travels, to places like Africa and India, which had a deep effect on him. He had an open heart and an open mind, which endeared him to so many people. I find this inspiring and uplifting.

All of these attributes appeal very much to me in a person. He is a shining example of how to make the very best out of the hand that life has dealt you, something I try to apply to my own life when things don't work out as expected.

He was fearless, which is why he was able to fly his own plane, skydive, surf, and so much more. I totally admire this as I am such a scaredy-cat!

He was just a cowboy at heart; he loved nature and animals as I do too. His beautiful ranch and horses are a testament to this and brought him so much joy on a personal level. I feel a common bond with Patrick on this and many other things in his life, including his spiritual side, which he spoke openly about when he was sick, acknowledging the presence of his dad around him. I like to believe he is still here in spirit and I hope he can feel the love that still exists for him.

He loved his fans and always, always made time for them no matter where he was in the world.

I wish I could have met him.

He was flawed just like the rest of us, struggling with addictions and emotional distress. Having fame and fortune and being a Hollywood heartthrob doesn't protect you from any of that. He wore his heart on his sleeve for sure, while most people in his position would be guarded and defensive.

Having read about his life and hearing stories from people who knew him, I would say he inspires me to be the best I can be, no matter what obstacles are thrown in front of me—to be true to myself and confident in my own ability, to accept my flaws as well as my strengths. Nobody is perfect, not even a jaw-dropping gorgeous Hollywood heartthrob! And never ever give up!

Basically, Patrick is very much the kind of person I would love to have in my circle of friends: a genuinely nice human being, funny and energetic, caring and compassionate, a man with a big heart and a small ego despite his fame and fortune. I think we would have a lot of common interests, and lots to talk about if ever we had met, including his Irish ancestry.

I am in awe of his many talents, besides his acting: a dancer, singer, horse breeder, pilot, and rancher. I would never have known about these things in the early days. Oh, and did I mention he was stunningly gorgeous? I mean, what's not to love?

Credit: Rick Smith/ Used with permission of the Music Hall Center for the Performing Arts.

*Patrick Swayze speaking at the*
*2002 Complexions Gala in Detroit, Michigan.*

CHAPTER THIRTEEN

## MY THOUGHTS AS TO WHAT PATRICK
## WOULD SAY TO US NOW

*Flash to 2018 to Patrick's Acceptance Speech for Receiving a Lifetime Achievement Award at the Academy Awards*
*\*This is a collage of Patrick's words that absolutely apply to today.*

"It's not the history making movies that is the reason I've had a thirty-year career—it's much longer than a thirty-year career when you think I came out of the womb on the stage! I've always had an uncanny knack whether it's a small movie or not, to find those characters, to find those roles even if they are dark characters to leave you out on the other end, that's changed you in some way or seeing things in another way or some level of identification that gets people to look from a different point of view. Usually I like it to be something that has to do with heart. . . .

Right now with this surface, shallow world of reality TV and everything worth believing in being devalued or laughed at, or if you have integrity 'What's wrong with you?' I'll never stop living my life by those clichés. You know, 'Only the strong survive,' 'Nobody said it would be easy,' 'Back up your mouth' and 'Give all you can because it will be returned.'"

"The dance world teaches you something. . . . The concept of: Suffer for your art. Pay your dues. And then it takes me into Texas clichés: Only the strong survive. Nobody said it was going to be easy. If it's worth having, it's worth working for. I live by these things in my life."

"I now live my life by most of the things my dad taught me. I think my favorite saying of his would be: 'All I got is my integrity. To this day, I ain't never seen a hearse pulling a U-Haul.'"

"I have to have a sense of passion and purpose in my life or the little bird dies inside of me. And I think it's all of our jobs to keep that little bird of innocence alive and to keep the cynicism out 'cause the world wants to make us all very, very cynical and destroy everything that is worth believing in. Even movies now are starting to attack our faith."

"Hopefully, with all of this reality TV mentality and the world going for nothing but anything that's surface, I hope that changes soon. I hope our standards, our levels of integrity and morality and passion and beliefs upgrade themselves soon."

"Very early I learned that you have to be true to yourself about what you care about—what you believe in. If you're not, you have nothing at all. You have to listen to that little bird inside that tells you what's right."

"When you look at the United States, the United States are systematically eliminating artistic classes for kids! It's insanity. We're going to build generations of computers, soul-less computers. People don't realise that nurturing that side of ourselves, nurturing that compassion, and that ephemeral and keeping that little bird alive and the child alive, which is the only way that we resist cynicism and becoming jaded. Those are the things that nurture our passion about preservation, conservation, everything. It's like the basis of where the goodness in us began and the hope continues."

"We kind of get ruined in the Western world of thinking that the brass ring is what's important, when it's very simple things in life that are important—like hanging on to faith and hope."

"I think we all need to remember that dreams are the fabric of the future and if you believe in those dreams, you can make them happen or re-discover an old dream. And just believe in yourself. And spread the love!"

# CLOSING

I had the wonderful opportunity to ask a question (via telephone) to Patrick on the CNBC *The Big Idea with Donny Deutsch Show* of May 25, 2005:

**Q: In one of your other movies [*One Last Dance*], Patrick, you play a character, Travis, who realizes his dreams. Do you feel you have realized your dreams? And what dreams do you still have left?**

A: Patrick: I've realized a lot of dreams, and you know, there is some truth to the way to screw someone's life up is to give them what they want. But in terms of dreams, it's a scary thing to achieve them because you've got a couple of options, either just more of the same, or you have to constantly reinvent, recreate, and come up with a new bigger dream. And I think that's key for all of us: *Don't give up where we're at.* That's what our movie *One Last Dance* is completely about, that moment in time when we give up on a dream. We have to get to realize that it's never too late to re-discover a dream or make up a new one.

# CANCER ORGANIZATIONS

**THE PATRICK SWAYZE PANCREAS CANCER RESEARCH FUND AT THE STANFORD CANCER INSTITUTE**
Stanford University Development Services
PO Box 20466
Stanford, CA 94309-0466
650-725-2504
**https://giving.Stanford.edu/goto/medgift**
*Type into the special instructions on the web form or write on memo line of check: Patrick Swayze Pancreas Cancer Research Fund or the fund code: GHBQQ.

**PANCREATIC CANCER ACTION NETWORK**
1500 Rosecrans Avenue, Suite 200
Manhattan Beach, CA 90266
877-272-6226 or 310-725-0025
**www.pancan.org**

**STAND UP TO CANCER**
File 1224 1801 W. Olympic Boulevard
Pasadena, CA 91199-1224
888-907-8263
**www.standup2cancer.org**

**AMERICAN CANCER SOCIETY**
PO Box 22718
Oklahoma City, OK 73123-1718
800-227-2345
**www.cancer.org**

*Sue Tabashnik*

## LEUKEMIA & LYMPHOMA SOCIETY
1311 Mamaroneck Avenue, Suite 310
White Plains, NY 10605
888-557-7177
**www.lls.org**

# ACKNOWLEDGMENTS

It is with the utmost gratitude that I thank the many, many people who provided support, love, and expertise to me that allowed me to write this book.

First of all, I thank my family, especially my mom, Phyllis Friedman, my dad, David Tabashnik—both who are always with me in spirit; my brothers, Bruce Tabashnik and David Tabashnik, my aunts, Nedra Kapetansky and Mary Lou Zieve; my nephew Gabe Tabashnik, Andrea Mathis, and cousins Carol and Mike Golob, and Joanne Canvasser.

A special thank-you to Margaret Howden, a dear friend who is president of the Official Patrick Swayze International Fan Club and publisher/editor of the Official Patrick Swayze International Fan Club magazine. I so appreciate your support, time, and access to the many invaluable materials from the club: the transcript and video of the 2007 holiday message, the 2007 London interview of Patrick, the Complexions gala photos, and much more.

A special thank-you to my dear friend Joshua Sinclair. I so appreciate your support, time, invaluable feedback on the manuscript, the tribute to Patrick, and use of the materials from *Jump!* including excerpts from the press kit and the numerous, wonderful photos.

A special thank-you to my dear friends Mary Kiriazis and Michelle Tukel, who always stand by me, through thick and thin.

I know Bob Howell and Lee Santiwan are with me in spirit, and yes, a third book.

I thank my dear friend Jackie Horner for always supporting my writing and for her role in creating and perpetuating the *Dirty Dancing* story.

I thank my dear friend, Don Frazier for instilling in me the "body-building/warrior spirit."

I thank my health care providers for hanging in there with me, especially Dr. O, Dr. F, Dr. Yashinsky, Dr. Elkiss, Dr. Faila, Laurie Saunders, John Gifford, and James Watson.

I thank my book maven/designer, Patricia Bacall, and editors extraordinaire, Pamela Cangioli and Kimberley Jace.

I thank my expert attorney, Larry Jordan, who never tired of my endless questions.

I deeply acknowledge the generosity and graciousness of sharing information and time of Jordan Brady, Eleanor Bergstein, Linda Gottlieb, Piper Laurie, Marshall R. Teague, Diane Venora, Scott Wilder, Tom Sanders, Alex Simon, Joe Leydon, Bobbie Wygant, Elliott Sharp, Xav Judd, Karl J. Paloucek, Randee Dawn, Andrew Dansby, Jan Griffith, Catherine, Patt and Tom Rocks, Betty Rollins, Mike Porterfield, Patricia Mendoza, and Vince Paul.

I send a big thank-you to the following media for permission for use of their material: BBC, *The Boston Globe*, *Channel Guide Magazine*, CNBC, *Daily Mail*, Guardian News & Media Ltd, *The Houston Chronicle*, *Mother Nature Network*, NBC-Today.com, NPR, *Orange Coast*, St. Martin's Press, and *US Weekly*. I thank Martha McClintock at Getty Images.

I send a big shout-out to my many, many supportive work colleagues and gym buddies.

# PERMISSIONS

I gratefully thank these sources for giving permission to use their material.

## CHAPTER ONE

"Lisa: Merry Christmas": Used with permission of the Official Patrick Swayze International Fan Club. Video Interview of Patrick Swayze and Lisa Niemi. London. November 27, 2005.

"Actually, at age thirteen, I made a big decision": © 2005 by CNBC. *The Big Idea with Donny Deutsch*. Courtesy of CNBC. May 25, 2005.

"He really taught me": © 2004 by *Venice Magazine*. "PATRICK SWAYZE: PEACEFUL WARRIOR." Alex Simon. June 2004. Re-published June 10, 2015 in "Great Conversations: Patrick Swayze." Alex Simon. Co-editor. The Hollywood Interview.

"That's the other side of me": © 2004 by *Venice Magazine*. Alex Simon. Ibid.

## CHAPTER TWO

"I was literally born under the stage": © 2006 by BBC. *HARDtalk Extra*. Gavin Esler. 2006.

"He wants to be a star": © 1987 by Joe Leydon. "Patrick Swayze: 'Dancing' on top of the world." The Moving Picture. August 19, 1987.

"But Swayze has tamed": © 1987 by Joe Leydon. Ibid.

"As to Patrick": © 2013 by Sue Tabashnik. Updated version of quote from Linda Gottlieb interview in *The Fans' Love Story*

*ENCORE: How the Movie* DIRTY DANCING *Captured the Hearts of Millions*! by Sue Tabashnik. Passion Spirit Dreams Press. 2013.

"The only actor ever": © 2017 by NBC. "'Dirty Dancing' turns 30: Here are 6 things to know about the '80s classic." Randee Dawn. January 25, 2017. TODAY.com. Used with edits by and permission of Eleanor Bergstein.

"The dance world teaches": © 2006 by BBC. *HARDtalk Extra*. Gavin Esler. 2006.

"Like Zucker, Kidron": © 1995 by *US Weekly LLC*. "Patrick Swayze-The US Interview." Tom O'Neill. September 1995. All rights reserved. Used with permission.

"Kidron insists that": © 1995 by Joe Leydon. "Patrick Swayze: Getting in touch with his feminine side as a most womanly woman in 'To Wong Foo.'" The Moving Picture. September 3, 1995.

"But I am really hellbent": © 1995 by Joe Leydon. Ibid.

"Q: Why not reprise": © 2005 by *Globe Newspaper Company*. "Stayin' Alive." Mark Shanahan. *The Boston Globe*. September 29, 2005.

"How do you decide": © 2005 by Xav Judd. "INTERVIEW WITH PATRICK SWAYZE." November 25, 2005.

"I just realised that": Used with permission of the Official Patrick Swayze International Fan Club. Interview of Patrick Swayze. November 27, 2005.

"Very early I learned": From *PATRICK SWAYZE* © 1988 by Mitchell Krugel. Reprinted by permission of St. Martin's Press. All rights reserved.

"The people really affected me": © 2004 by *Channel Guide Magazine*. "Swayze's dance card is plenty full these days." Karl J. Paloucek. June 6, 2004.

"This is my keepsake": © 1995 by *US Weekly LLC*. "Patrick

Swayze-The US Interview." September 1995. Tom O'Neill. All rights reserved. Used with permission.

"I don't care what": © 1995 by *US Weekly LLC*. Ibid.

"It's like, not a whole lot": © 1995 by Joe Leydon. "Patrick Swayze: Getting in touch with his feminine side as a most womanly woman in 'To Wong Foo.'" The Moving Picture. September 3, 1995.

"It's not so much about trying": © 1995 by *US Weekly LLC*. Patrick Swayze-The US Interview. Tom O'Neill. September 1995. All rights reserved. Used with permission.

"In fact, he closely resembled Dalton": © 2015 by Alex Simon. "Great Conversations: Patrick Swayze." Alex Simon. June 10, 2015. Co-editor. The Hollywood Interview.

"The whole basis of *Road House*": © 2004 by *Venice Magazine*. "PATRICK SWAYZE: PEACEFUL WARRIOR." Alex Simon. June 2004. Re-published June 10, 2015 in "Great Conversations: Patrick Swayze." Alex Simon. Co-editor. The Hollywood Interview.

"I feel it really turned out to be": Used with permission from the archives of bobbiewygant.com. Bobbie Wygant, a long-time entertainment reporter and critic with NBC 5 KXAS-TV Channel 5 Dallas/Fort Worth.

"It has been so successful": © 2006 by Guardian News & Media Ltd. "Patrick Swayze on 'Dirty Dancing.'" Telegraph.co.uk. September 23, 2006.

"I've always had the desire": © 2006 by BBC. *HARDtalk Extra*. Gavin Esler. 2006.

"Like John Travolta": © 2009 by *Houston Chronicle*. "Swayze was bridge from musicals to teen movies." Andrew Dansby. September 14, 2009.

"From his screen debut in *Skatetown*": © 2015 by Alex Simon. "Great Conversations: Patrick Swayze." Alex Simon. June 10, 2015. Co-editor. The Hollywood Interview.

"There's a moment where": © 2009 by NPR. "Swayze's Dancing Brought Characters to Life." NPR. Jesse Baker. September 15, 2009. Quote by Carrie Rickey (*Philadelphia Inquirer*).

"Everybody knows we lost": © 2013 by Vice Media. "Patrick Swayze-The Lost Tapes." Elliott Sharp. Noisey.com. April 2013.

"We'd be fools to believe": © 2013 by Vice Media. Elliott Sharp. Ibid.

"Everywhere we take this film": © 2005 by *Globe Newspaper Company*. "Stayin' Alive." Mark Shanahan. *The Boston Globe*. September 29, 2005.

"The world loves dance": © 2005 by *Globe Newspaper Company*. Ibid.

"For so many years": © 2004 by *Orange Coast* magazine. "Power of One." Greg Hernandez. July 2004 (Volume 30, Number 7).

"OFC: Are there any amusing": © 2000 by the Official Patrick Swayze International Fan Club. Interview of Jordan Brady, 2000. Used with permission of Jordan Brady.

"He was an incredible, tough guy": © 2017 by Sue Tabashnik. Interview of Scott Wilder. January 8, 2017.

"He was very nice to the extras": © 2013 by Sue Tabashnik. Interview of Tom and Patt Rocks in *The Fans' Love Story ENCORE: How the Movie DIRTY DANCING Captured the Hearts of Millions!* Passion Spirit Dreams Press.

"I'll tell you about Buddy": © 2010 by Sue Tabashnik. Interview of Mike Porterfield in *The Fans' Love Story: How the Movie DIRTY DANCING Captured the Hearts of Millions!* Outskirts Press.

"It's not the history making movies": Used with permission of the Official Patrick Swayze International Fan Club. Interview of Patrick Swayze. November 27, 2005.

## CHAPTER THREE

"He [Patrick] knows the new film": © 1987 by Joe Leydon. "Patrick Swayze: 'Dancing' on top of the world." The Moving Picture. August 19, 1987.

"Swayze says, 'I began to see": © 1995 by Joe Leydon. "Patrick Swayze: Getting in touch with his feminine side as a most womanly woman in 'To Wong Foo.'" The Moving Picture. September 3, 1995.

"It was my opportunity to": © 2004 by *Orange Coast* magazine. "Power of One." Greg Hernandez. July 2004 (Volume 30, Number 7).

"A true story": © 2008 by Joshua Sinclair. Press kit for *Jump!*

"We do not know for sure": © 2016 by Joshua Sinclair as told to Sue Tabashnik. July 19, 2016.

"The Best of *The Beast*": © 2009 by Jan Griffith. Featured in the August 2009 Official Patrick Swayze International Fan Club Magazine.

## CHAPTER FOUR

"Relationships are hard": © 2004 by *Orange Coast* magazine. "Power of One." Greg Hernandez. July 2004 (Volume 30, Number 7).

"That's not to say": © 2005 by *Daily Mail*. "Drink, suicide and why I turned against Hollywood." Lester Middlehurst. November 29, 2005.

"Were you attracted to the idea": © 2005 by Xav Judd. "INTERVIEW WITH PATRICK SWAYZE." November 25, 2005.

"He was a gentle soul": © 2005 by *Daily Mail*. "Drink, suicide and why I turned against Hollywood." Lester Middlehurst. November 29, 2005.

"Her death changed my life": © 2005 by *Daily Mail*. Lester Middlehurst. Ibid.

## CHAPTER FIVE

"And, you know": © 2013 by Sue Tabashnik. Interview of Jackie Horner in *The Fans' Love Story ENCORE: How the Movie* DIRTY DANCING *Captured the Hearts of Millions!* by Sue Tabashnik. Passion Spirit Dreams Press. 2013.

"But, you know, I don't consider *Dirty Dancing*": © 1987 by Joe Leydon. "Patrick Swayze: 'Dancing' on top of the world." The Moving Picture. August 19, 1987.

"After we finished the major push": Used with permission of the Official Patrick Swayze International Fan Club. Interview of Patrick Swayze. November 27, 2005.

## CHAPTER SIX

"I now have ten years": Used with permission of the Official Patrick Swayze International Fan Club. Ibid.

"I feel it's completely and totally who I am": © 2004 by *Channel Guide Magazine*. "Swayze's dance card is plenty full these days." Karl J. Paloucek. June 6, 2004.

"He also heavily supported": © 2009 by *Mother Nature Network*. "Patrick Swayze remembered for conservation efforts." Katy Rank Lev. September 21, 2009.

## CHAPTER NINE

"I love seeing if I can": © 2005 by CNBC. *The Big Idea with Donny Deutsch*. Courtesy of CNBC. May 25, 2005.

"Fans have been so faithful": © 2004 by *Orange Coast* magazine. "Power of One." Greg Hernandez. July 2004 (Volume 30, Number 7).

**CHAPTER ELEVEN**

"Second in a Lifetime Opportunity": © 2003 by Sue Tabashnik. Featured in the Official Patrick Swayze International Fan Club Magazine.

**CHAPTER THIRTEEN**

"It's not the history making movies": Used with permission of the Official Patrick Swayze International Fan Club. Interview of Patrick Swayze. November 27, 2005.

"The dance world teaches you something": © 2006 by BBC. *HARDtalk Extra*. Gavin Esler. 2006.

"I now live my life by most": © 2004 by *Venice Magazine*. "PATRICK SWAYZE: PEACEFUL WARRIOR." Alex Simon. June 2004. Re-published June 10, 2015, in "Great Conversations: Patrick Swayze." Alex Simon. Co-editor. The Hollywood Interview.

"I have to have a sense of passion": © 2006 by BBC. *HARDtalk Extra*. Gavin Esler. 2006.

"Hopefully, with all of this reality TV mentality": © 2006 by BBC. *HARDtalk Extra*. Gavin Esler. 2006.

"Very early I learned": From *PATRICK SWAYZE* © 1988 by Mitchell Krugel. Reprinted by permission of St. Martin's Press. All rights reserved.

"When you look at the United States": Used with permission of the Official Patrick Swayze International Fan Club. Interview of Patrick Swayze. November 27, 2005.

"We kind of get ruined": © 2004 by *Channel Guide Magazine*. "Swayze's dance card is plenty full these days." Karl J. Paloucek. June 6, 2004.

"I think we all need to remember": Used with permission of the Official Patrick Swayze International Fan Club. Video Interview of Patrick Swayze and Lisa Niemi. London. November 27, 2005.

## CLOSING

"In one of your other movies": © 2005 by CNBC. *The Big Idea with Donny Deutsch*. Courtesy of CNBC. May 25, 2005.

Credit: Murray Goldenberg.

## ABOUT THE AUTHOR

**S**ue Tabashnik published two unique *Dirty Dancing* tribute books, *The Fans' Love Story: How the Movie* DIRTY DANCING *Captured the Hearts of Millions!* (July 2010) and *The Fans' Love Story ENCORE: How the Movie* DIRTY DANCING *Captured the Hearts of Millions!* (December 2013). She became a fan of Patrick Swayze in 1988. She was an active member of the Official Patrick Swayze International Fan Club from 2000–2010, which included writing numerous articles for the club magazine. She had the good fortune to meet Patrick Swayze several times at movie screenings and benefit events from 2002–2004, which led her to become an even bigger fan. Sue has worked as a master's level social worker since 1977. She has lived most of her life in the Detroit area.

*Author website:* www.likedirtydancing.com

**In memory of my grandmother, Leah Tabashnik, and Patrick Swayze: A portion of the proceeds from the sale of this book will be donated to the Patrick Swayze Pancreas Cancer Research Fund at the Stanford Cancer Institute.**